Angel Whispers

Angel Whispers

How to Get Closer to your Angels

Jenny Smedley

HAY HOUSE

Australia • Canada • Hong Kong • India
South Africa • United Kingdom • United States

PREVIOUS BOOKS BY JENNY SMEDLEY

Past Life Meditation, CD, M2 Productions, 2004

Past Life Angels, O Books, 2005

Souls Don't Lie, O Books, 2006

The Tree That Talked, O Books, 2007

The Night of the Unicorn, with Tony Smedley,
O Books, 2008

How to Be Happy, O Books, 2008

Pets Have Souls Too, Hay House, 2009

First published and distributed in the United Kingdom by:

Hay House UK Ltd, 292B Kensal Rd, London W10 5BE. Tel.: (44) 20 8962 1230; Fax: (44) 20 8962 1239. www.hayhouse.co.uk

Published and distributed in the United States of America by:

Hay House, Inc., PO Box 5100, Carlsbad, CA 92018-5100. Tel.: (1) 760 431 7695 or (800) 654 5126; Fax: (1) 760 431 6948 or (800) 650 5115. www.hayhouse.com

Published and distributed in Australia by:

Hay House Australia Ltd, 18/36 Ralph St, Alexandria NSW 2015. Tel.: (61) 2 9669 4299; Fax: (61) 2 9669 4144. www.hayhouse.com.au

Published and distributed in the Republic of South Africa by:

Hay House SA (Pty), Ltd, PO Box 990, Witkoppen 2068. Tel./Fax: (27) 11 467 8904. www.hayhouse.co.za

Published and distributed in India by:

Hay House Publishers India, Muskaan Complex, Plot No.3, B-2, Vasant Kunj, New Delhi – 110 070. Tel.: (91) 11 4176 1620; Fax: (91) 11 4176 1630. www.hayhouse.co.in

Distributed in Canada by:

Raincoast, 9050 Shaughnessy St, Vancouver, BC V6P 6E5. Tel.: (1) 604 323 7100; Fax: (1) 604 323 2600

A catalogue record for this book is available from the British Library.

ISBN 978-1-84850-154-6

Printed and bound in Great Britain by CPI Bookmarque, Croydon CR0 4TD

I'd like to dedicate this book to all the people in the world, both living and passed to spirit, who have ever shown me love.

You don't need wings to be able to fly — you just need the help of someone who can fly.

JENNY SMEDLEY

CONTENTS

ACKNOWLEDGEMENTS

I thank my angels for sharing my life.
I'd also like to thank Michelle and everyone at
Hay House for their faith in me.
As always, I thank my soulmate and husband
Tony for all his support.

INTRODUCTION

Why have I written this book? Quite simply, I was featured in an article in the *Daily Mail* about angels recently and I received a staggering number of e-mails in response to it, all asking the same thing: 'How can I get closer to my angels?' There's no quick answer to this. It can't be written in an e-mail. So this book has been written in answer to all those people who e-mailed me and all the others in the world who'd like to know the answer to the same question.

There are many reasons why you might have been drawn to pick up this book in particular. You might have liked the cover, the colours and the design. You might have read the back cover and been impressed with what was said there, or an endorsement from someone you admire might have made you pick it up. You might be fed up with the shallow behaviour of some of the people you meet and want to find a way to change the world. You might be facing difficult times – redundancies, ill health, relationship issues – and be asking, 'Is this all there is or can I tap into more?' You might be one of those who realize that the world's consciousness is changing, *has* to change, and want to become a drop of water in the glass of goodness that we need to dose the planet and its people with. It really doesn't matter what drew you to this book, because whatever it was, it will have been created by your angels' energy, pulling you towards them.

You might have opened this book looking for help but be wondering, 'Why should I trust what's written here?' My answer to this question is: 'Because I'm a living example of how angels *can* take action to change your life, even when it seems there is no hope, and I want to help you see how to achieve the same thing.'

It *can* be done. Your life *can* be changed. I'm showing you a way to get closer to angels that's possible for every single person. It will take perseverance and commitment, but it's not a quick-fix pill like a bad diet that fails a few weeks later, it's a change for *life*. It will lead you to a new way of *being*.

When I was a child, I was able to connect with my Guardian Angel quite easily, as most young children can, although of course I had no idea at the time that that's what I was doing. At that age, everything was light and bright and the feelings I had when angels were around were natural and just accepted as normal.

I remember once when I was about three years old, my mum took me to catch a train to my auntie's hotel in Southsea. I didn't really like the panting steam engines as they were huge and noisy, like dragons that might eat a little girl right up. We had to change trains in London and after finding the right platform we got into an empty compartment on our connecting train and sat down. But as the train started to slowly grind its way out of the station, the announcer's voice informed Mum she'd got on the wrong train and we were headed in completely the wrong direction, towards Brighton!

Naturally a bit panic-stricken, Mum opened the train door (they didn't lock in those days) and got ready to jump back down onto the platform. She told me in a firm voice, 'Wait right there, I'll catch you,' and she jumped off, intending to turn around immediately and whisk me from the doorway. But in my little three-year-old mind all I knew was that my mum had jumped off, the train was moving faster and we were being separated. Mum had stumbled slightly as she had landed on what was, to her, moving ground, but she would have been able to grab me I'm sure, even if she'd had to run down the platform alongside the train to do so. But I wasn't waiting, no way was I going to get carried away from my mum by the monster, and so I launched myself off the train with no idea of what would happen next, just that I'd be with my mum.

In hindsight, it was very dangerous. I could have fallen on landing and slipped under the train, as the gap in those days between platform and train was quite wide. The train was also going fast enough by then for me to have been hurt in the fall.

As I jumped, I could see no one on the platform except my mum. I remember her petrified eyes looking back at me as she ran towards me, but she would never have reached me before I hit the platform. However, I was completely unafraid of falling. A part of me just knew that I was protected and that I wouldn't be hurt. All I was afraid of was losing my mum.

Suddenly I could feel the warmth of what I now know were my Guardian's wings holding me gently. I seemed to float and time stood still, but I wasn't surprised. Then, with a rush, I was grabbed out of midair and swung around in a porter's strong arms. I have no idea where he came from. He handed me back to my relieved mum with a stern admonishment never to do anything so silly again.

Everyone seemed stunned that I wasn't hurt. But I'd known I was safe. I also knew that someone besides the porter had saved me, but back then I didn't know who.

Of course, as with most children, the pressure of peers and of growing up soon divorced me from that happy natural union with my Guardian Angel, and it took me many years to be aware of his presence again, although I know he never left. It was I who left – in my mind, anyway.

Demonstrating how our lives are mapped out to an extent, when I was 12 years old angels also saved my future husband, Tony, from accidental death, in order that we would one day be together, as we were destined to be. Without his love and support I would never have found my life path. I met him when I was 17 and he was 19, five years after his accident. This year, 2009, we'll have been married for 40 years, as we married when I was 19 and he was 21.

The accident Tony had, which really should have been fatal, happened when he was 14. He was cycling to school with a couple of friends down the road that led to the nearby Shell Refinery, a journey he'd done countless times before. On that day the road was a little icy and, perhaps distracted by that and by the wind of a passing oil tanker, Tony thinks he clipped the back wheel of his friend's cycle with his own front wheel. The next thing he knew he was sliding towards the tanker's back wheels, and then there was only blackness until he woke up in a hospital bed, miraculously suffering from nothing more than severe concussion. No one could explain how he could have been struck on the head by the wheel of a hugely heavy vehicle doing a fairly fast speed, and survived. Literally a few inches' difference and he would have been killed, especially when you consider that those tankers had double sets of wheels at the back.

What made it even more of a miracle was that the driver of the tanker had glanced in his side mirror and seen Tony falling under his wheels. He'd instinctively pulled the steering wheel away from him, but of course, as he was towing a long trailer, this would actually have taken the back wheels even closer to Tony. So there is no doubt that something or someone placed him exactly where he needed to be in order to just get lightly clipped and survive falling under the tanker's wheels.

As I said, I grew up and gained a marvellous husband, but along the way I lost the connection to my Guardian

Angel, lost the knowledge and lost the faith, and started to drift, to the point where, some 15 years ago, I was in a very bad place. Despite my happy marriage, I could see no future for myself, because I felt there was something missing, something I should have been doing, but I had no clue what it was. I felt useless and rudderless, and I was almost at the point of suicide. I can honestly say that if it hadn't been for Tony and our son, I might well have taken that route. I was only 45, yet I could see nothing ahead but a downhill slope. But what the angels actually had in store for me was beyond my imagination!

I'd been brought up a Catholic but defected from that religion many years previously through becoming disillusioned. Like most people I really wished for things, prayed for things, searched for a purpose and became desperate when none of my wishes came true and it seemed that none of my prayers was ever answered.

As a family we were also in some financial difficulties, which didn't help. I hadn't worked for years and had lost the confidence to even try to get a job. I had no talent and no skills that I was aware of. I was a hypochondriac, with mysterious and scary pains, and I had a lifelong phobia of flying. I didn't like the way things were, but I was scared of change – scared of everything really, even life itself. I'd been eating and eating to comfort myself and become very overweight, which only added to my woes and lack of self-esteem, and that was when the worst thing ever happened – my mum died. She'd been the centre of everything in my wider family and without her, that support structure fell apart.

I thought I'd hit bottom at that point, but I carried on sinking for another four years, until I found myself one day sitting alone, feeling fat and unnecessary and wondering if I should bother carrying on, and that's when everything suddenly changed. I'd heard of people who'd said their whole lives had changed in an instant and doubted it was possible, but I was about to find out that it was.

If, at that moment, an angel had chosen to appear and had told me that over the course of the next 15 years I would write an award-winning song, lose three stone and become healthy, present my own TV show for two years, have 11 books published and fly to America not once but three times, I would have laughed hysterically in its face. All these things did indeed come to pass, but not until I learned to how to listen to angels, and even then not in any way I could have imagined. As time went by, I learned to communicate with angels and, most important of all, I was shown my purpose in this life by an angel.

In order to hear and be heard by an angel that can really change things for you, you have to raise your vibrations, and in the following chapters I'll be discussing what this means and how to do it in a balanced way. I sometimes feel that severe depression is actually quite close to meditation, which does raise your vibrations, and that's why it's often when we're at our lowest that at last we hear the voice of an angel. When we are depressed we stop caring about the material world, or life in general, which is often our greatest block, and this sometimes opens us up in a way that we haven't known how to achieve before. That's what happened to me, the depression opened me up, but you won't have to travel that path. This book is designed to help you in a much more comfortable way.

In my case, at that lowest moment of my life I heard a voice clearly in my head. No flourish of angelic trumpets or great message for the world, just a voice saying, 'Turn the TV on.' Angels work in mysterious ways!

I obeyed this odd directive, because by that time I had no mind of my own. And at that moment, when I looked at the screen, I was suddenly awakened to my past lives, because I recognized a stranger on the television. And something about him removed my deep depression in an instant.

At the time I didn't know why this miracle had occurred, I was just joyous that it had. It was another six months before I understood what was going on. During those six months I just rested, bathing in unaccustomed happiness and buoyed up by the encouraging presence that seemed to accompany me everywhere. Of course now I know that I had been made aware of the presence of my Guardian Angel. It was a gentle time, and I was still fairly rudderless, but it was also a time to awaken my creativity, and that's when I started writing songs. They poured out of me, but no one was more surprised than I was when they started to be recorded and one even won a silver disc for the artist. I wondered whether songwriting was the future and purpose I'd been searching for, but that wasn't the case, the songs were just one step on my journey.

Six months later I realized that it was connecting to a past life that had woken me up and so I went for hypnotic regression to find out the full story. The realization that there was so much more to me than I'd previously thought changed my perspective on life in general and my life in particular. On my insistence Tony gave up his stressful job, we sold our small farm and upped sticks, virtually overnight, following some direction or call to move to the hills of Somerset. In hindsight it all seemed very reckless, but by then I'd started to dream of angels and to meditate, and I was obeying every message I got, whether it came in a dream or as a waking vision during meditation.

A few months later, as I was journeying across country on a train, I decided to 'switch off' with a deep meditation. I slipped away from the world around me, the noise and bustle of the train receding along with it. Then suddenly I found myself in the presence of a wondrous being. It stretched to the stars and beyond and yet it was all right there in front of me and I could see it easily. It glowed with a light that was golden and yet richer than molten gold. This light was more dazzling than the sun, much too bright to gaze at without becoming blind, and yet I could look right at it. It had no real recognizable form, and yet it was instantly familiar and welcome.

I've searched many times for the words to describe how it actually *feels* to be in the presence of an angel and I've failed utterly. 'Rapture' is the only word that comes close. There is a love both given and received that transcends anything I've ever experienced as a human, and as I love my husband more than life, that is really saying something. When this angel showed me my path, which was to be a spiritual seed-planter, and offered it to me if I was willing to take it on (it did not command me), I accepted the role gratefully, knowing nothing would make me happier than to cooperate with this 'Master Path Angel'.

In the following months the angel started to give me the abilities that I'd need to carry out my 'job' successfully. A lot of talents were downloaded at night, and Tony got used to me suddenly sitting bolt upright in bed and scribbling things down on a notepad that I soon learned to keep right by the bed. These talents included the ability to do digital angel artwork readings, remote aura photos and readings (where I change ordinary photos into aura photos) and also spirit guide portraits, none of which I'd been able to do before. Soon, out of the blue, I was offered a job at our local TV station and before long I was producing and presenting a daily chat show on spiritual matters that ran for two years. Later I was led to various magazines and asked to write columns and articles for them, and I now do magazine columns worldwide. In 2004 I was approached by a small publisher and asked to start writing books seriously. Finally I got to where I am today, satisfying the Master Path

Angel by seed-planting and satisfying my lifelong ambition to earn a living with my writing.

Over the years I've learned of many paths to angels. On my TV show I've interviewed countless experts on the subject and many people who have had their own angelically influenced journey. I've talked to those who have been saved from drug-induced suicide or accident by an angel and, like me, have heard a short few words that have changed their life. I've tried many angel therapies and many of the tools that are out there for connecting to angels, and found out which ones work and which don't. I've learned how to get in touch with angels and what to ask for when I do, and I'd like to share these experiences with you.

You might well ask why it's so hard to connect to angels. Why isn't it as easy as picking up the phone? That would make life easier, but it wouldn't be right. We come here in human form to face a challenge. If we succeed, then our souls are free to move on; and if we don't, then it's back to the drawing board and back in another life. The challenge we face is this: we come to this life fragmented, our mind, body and soul disunited. We have to find a way to reunite these facets of ourselves into a spiritual unity, while enduring all that is human, which naturally pulls us away from such things.

When we're very young we don't have this problem, but as we get older our parents' attempts to mould us into socially acceptable people, our teachers' attempts to fit us into boxes and our partners' attempts to change us to suit them better all drive a wedge between our mind, body and soul and drive us away from spirituality. These people all mean well, but their influence doesn't make it easy to reconnect to what's really important, which is not the accumulation of money or material property, or success, celebrity or power.

If we wake up to our spirituality and become perfectly blended, then life does indeed become easier, though. For instance dis-ease becomes a thing of the past as our minds have total control over our bodies and our innate ability to heal ourselves means no illness is allowed to take over. By reuniting soul with mind and body in perfect balance we are able to raise our energy vibrations enough to connect with other dimensions and this is where we can talk to higher angels, who have the power to alter our life path. Once on our rightful path we become happy and successful, though not necessarily in the material way measured by our world's yardstick.

It sounds wonderful, doesn't it, but I have to give you one word of warning. I am truly blessed, and my life is amazing, but it isn't perfect. Life isn't *meant* to be perfect – we're all here to learn, and some lessons come through adversity. So I can't promise you the perfect life with no problems whatsoever. What I can and do promise is to show you a way to better your life and gain fulfilment, which is what creates true happiness and the strength to cope with the trials of the human condition. It isn't easy, but with faith, perseverance and determination, you too can get closer to your angels. What follows is a route-map based on my own experiences. It offers a path to happiness that anyone can aspire to.

CHAPTER 1
WHAT ARE ANGELS?

A definition is always a good place to start – that way you know what you're dealing with! There have been many descriptions of angels down the centuries, but I'm going to stray a little from the norm here. I could write out a version of all the complicated hierarchies of angels as given in biblical or other religious texts, but really, in my experience, there are only four types of angels that you really need to know about while you're here on Earth. The others aren't there to communicate with us on a one-to-one basis and in my opinion it can often just confuse the issue if we try to reach them. After all, scientists say there could be 21 dimensions between our Guardian Angels and God, so there must be many beings that we'll never understand or come into contact with while we're still in the physical world.

My four categories of angels are: *Soul Angels* (or what I sometimes call *Past-Life Angels*), *Master Path Angels*, *Guardian Angels* and what I like to call *Odd Job Angels*.

Soul Angels are basically here to monitor your soul's progress through multiple lives and in between lives. This is a very large subject and will be better covered in a book of its own, so I won't go into it in great detail here, but let's take a look at the other types of angel.

ODD JOB ANGELS

This somewhat comical title suits these angels down to the ground. If I were to picture one in my mind it would probably look like a little fat winged cherub or something equally cute. These angels normally are unseen, though, except perhaps as the little black dots that you sometimes see zipping across the room out of the corner of your eye. They're sometimes called elementals or even fairies. They seem to be always hovering around us and I imagine them acting like a crowd of cheerful little brightly coloured butterflies flitting around a purple-bloomed buddleia bush, wanting to help us out in their own little ways.

These angels aren't able to accomplish real miracles or life-changing events, but they can give you immediate help in a trivial everyday situation. Most well known, for instance, is the 'car-parking angel'. In this day and age parking spaces are often at a premium, especially at times like Christmas, so it's a good idea to call on the help of the car-parking angel. I've done it so many times that I have no doubt whatsoever that it works. As soon as you leave home, start picturing the car park you're going to and simply ask that you be provided with a space. Every time I've done this, without fail, the most crowded of car parks has yielded up an empty spot within a few minutes, if not immediately.

I was once talking to a real sceptic about the car-parking angel and I made her laugh by saying, 'I'm glad you don't believe, because the more people that do, the more the car-parking spaces are going to be used up, and my Odd Job Angel will find it harder to get me one! We might end up with millions of little Odd Job Angels having "parking rage" battles all over the car parks!'

Two days later she told me that because of the joke I'd made she'd decided to call me on my claims and had deliberately gone to a very busy shopping centre – this was two weeks before Christmas – and, much to her surprise, after asking all the way there to find a space, she had driven straight into one that had been vacated just as she had pulled in.

Odd Job Angels also get you to the right place by clearing the traffic when you're about to be late for an appointment, or find lost items for you. Once when I'd lost our only back-door key in our eight-acre field of long grass while walking the dogs, I asked my Odd Job Angel for help in dowsing with my crystal for the key and found it within a dozen strides – seemingly an impossible task.

These angels are also sometimes good at repairing electrical devices. If something's broken, it's always worth asking for their help at bedtime, and if you're lucky, in the morning the device will work again.

GUARDIAN ANGELS

It's said that every single person has a specific Guardian Angel assigned to them and I've found this to be true. Your Guardian Angel is always around you and can change things in your life on an everyday level. They can sometimes be seen and can often speak to you as a little voice of reason or protect you from serious accidents that weren't meant to be, perhaps by delaying your journey or cautioning you to slow down in the car.

Graham, of Norwich in the UK, told me what happened to him:

I'd enjoyed a lovely day out in the country with the family and dog and we were driving home along the main road to Norwich. We were all feeling relaxed and happy and were bowling along in the car at roughly 60 miles an hour, none of us expecting any problems to crop up. But suddenly, as the car approached a blind bend, I heard a voice saying, 'Slow down!'

I felt a need to obey right away and it's a good job I did, because just round the bend there was a young girl standing in the middle of the road holding a pushbike. Because I'd slowed down I was able to stop in plenty of time and go round her, but if I hadn't listened to the voice in my head I would have definitely run her down and possibly killed her, which just goes to show that one must always listen to one's angels.

Guardian Angels can manipulate the physical world to a certain extent, perhaps giving you a shove to push you out of danger you weren't designed to meet, but their power is limited. Nevertheless these are very useful angels when it comes to solving some of your problems and creating a positive energy bubble to live in.

Jan de Avalon, also from Norwich, told me the story of how her Guardian Angel called on higher powers to save her life many years ago:

I was 17 years old and living in a basement flat beneath an antique shop in Northam Road, Southampton. At the time I had a number of part-time jobs locally and I used to help out in the shop selling antiques as well. I had a bed-sitting room and a kitchen that led to a small enclosed yard that in turn backed onto a railway embankment. The apartment was tiny, but all I really needed at the time. It suited me fine even though it often got used as a bit of a storeroom as well.

On this evening it was very, very cold, almost frosty. I tried to light the coal fire and then remembered that I needed to go to the corner shop. I went up the internal stairs and through the antique shop, because the dustbin men were coming in the morning and there was loads of rubbish piled up outside the front door of the flat.

When I came back I had a quick chat with the owner before he locked up. I went through the back room and down the stairs to my flat.

The fire still hadn't taken hold, so I started poking it. I still had the coat on that I had bought the day before. It was a very beautiful and unusual coat – cream and navy-blue diamonds in a Mary Quant style, knitted from thick pure wool.

There was still not much sign of life in the fire. All I got was a few fine sparks that floated up into the air. As I was rattling the poker, I looked to the side and I saw some big cans that I didn't recognize. While still poking the fire I reached over, picked one up and shook it, thinking, 'What's this?' It had no cap on and there were some cellulose thinners in it. I didn't know where it had come from.

Poking the fire had put sparks in the air; shaking the can of thinners now created fumes all around me. The sparks caught the fumes and I saw the air ignite. Then the flames shot back into the can and it went off like a bomb. My hand got most of the blast and my fingers were blown back. I was aware of the pain for only a moment and then I was completely on fire. As it had exploded, the bottom of the can had blown out and sprayed the cellulose thinners everywhere. The whole place just ignited in a massive great whirl of fire all around me. Luckily, I had been holding the can to one side. If I'd been holding it front of me it would have gone off in my face.

Although my wool coat didn't go up in flames, my stockings melted and my legs were badly burned. I patted myself as best I could, trying to stop myself from burning, and I knew I had to get out. I couldn't go out of the front door because of the rubbish and the back door led to the railway line and a 16-foot drop, so the only way out of the flat was through the shop. I went through the door that led to the stairs and it slammed shut behind me. I was out of the room but I was still on fire. I just collapsed at the foot of the stairs.

As I lay there I had an automatic astral projection. I felt as though I was in a fast car. I was accelerating extremely quickly and I could feel my astral body moving away from my physical body. It wasn't the tunnel experience that many people describe, it was like a vortex. I was being sucked up into a tornado of energy. I could hear wonderful sounds and unusual 'singing' and see amazing colours. I had a wonderful sensation of being set free. It felt lovely.

Then, as I was halfway up the stairs, I looked down and saw myself smouldering away and I thought I was dead. But it was cool. It felt really good. I could feel the vortex of energy moving around me and hear a whistling sound and I felt as though I was being comforted and wrapped in cotton wool.

Then I noticed a silvery blue translucent wave of energy pulsating and flowing from me to my body lying on the floor. I realized I was still connected to the physical body. 'That doesn't seem right,' I thought. 'I am here and I can think, yet my body is on the floor.' I realized then that I couldn't be dead and had to get back.

Suddenly an incredibly high-pitched whistling sound came in and a whole host of angelic beings just appeared

– though there was no individual angel or being, it was a multitude of vibrations and sensations all moving in and out of one another, all merging, with every colour you can imagine, translucent, rather like oil on water, not still, but continuously moving. Then the shapes started forming into beings and they looked huge. The whole area was filling up with amazing energy. It was all around my physical body and I could feel myself merging with it. It seemed that the angels had come to take me home.

In my awareness it was as though they said to me, 'We have come. We will assist you.' I can't remember all the words now, but I have never forgotten the last thing that was said: 'We will always remain with you.' With that, I felt as though my spiritual body had been absorbed completely into them like a sponge. I was completely with them and I felt enormous.

It was absolute bliss and pure love. I had merged into the amazing energy and I felt so safe, and yet something didn't feel right. I knew I was still linked to my physical body.

As I looked down at my physical body, I saw it was coming up off the ground. 'This can't be happening,' I thought. 'How can I move?' I had no essence, there was nothing inside my body because I was outside it, yet I saw it rising up as if it was being levitated. The angelic energy had lifted it from the ground.

Then I saw it coming up the stairs towards me. There was a whooshing sound and the angelic energy started moving away like a white cloud, leaving me there. I felt abso-

lutely enormous and wonderful. I felt so full of love and I didn't want to go back inside my body. 'No. I like it. This is lovely.'

But then, as I came together with my physical body, there was an incredible sensation. Remember when you were a child and blew through a straw into a drink and made hundreds of bubbles? It felt as though that was happening inside me, as if all my molecules were changing.

The next thing I knew, I was in my physical body again. I could see my legs were swelling up, blood was everywhere and my long hair was singed, but I felt no pain at all.

I don't remember walking up the rest of the stairs, but I do remember going through into the shop and looking at the front door. It was a plate-glass door and it was locked, but it was the only way out for me. I had to go through it.

I have no memory of smashing that door or doing anything to it. I just remember going through it and landing on my feet. It was as if I was in a dream state. The police later commented that the size of the hole in the door and the way the glass was broken didn't make sense. If something had been thrown through it, it would have shattered in a different way and if I had gone through the glass then I should have been badly cut, but there were no cuts on me. It was as if the hole had been made for me to leap through.

As my feet hit the ground, I suddenly came back to this reality. I heard a car screech and somebody saying, 'Oh, my God!' I still had smoke coming off me.

All I knew was that I had to get across that road and

to the people in the taxi rank opposite. *They were up a few steps. I was in total shock and it felt as though I was walking on sponge. When I got to the top of the stairs, there was a man polishing headlamps with some chrome cleaner. I just remember saying, 'Help.'*

He said, *'Oh, my God!' and ran over to me. He wrapped a big cloth all round my hand because my fingers were hanging off. He sat me down and the next thing that I remember was the ambulance people coming. They sat me in the ambulance and took me away. It was all such a haze.*

Eventually I came out of a semi-conscious state like a deep sleep and started to focus. I was in a special room in hospital. I had no clothes on and a cage over me with a blanket on top. My legs were open and raw. They had swelled up to two or three times their normal size. My hand was supported on a little table. I went to move, but I couldn't because I had drips in my arms. It was a terrible experience.

A policeman came and he was very nice. 'What are you doing causing a scene like this?' he said to me. 'They are going to take you to Odstock hospital. You're going to be all right. You're going to a special place. I've got your parents here with me.'

During all the months that I was recovering in hospital my father only came once and my mother came twice. But I had other visitors to look after me. My angels came to me many times. At night the energies would come and tap me on my head – a lovely feeling. I'd wake up immediately, so *alert. I know they weren't talking to me in the normal way, but I'd hear strange words inside my head, saying, 'You're going to be just fine. We'll be with you. We will never leave you. We are part of you. You are part of us.' I went on to make an extraordinary recovery.*

This account shows how Guardian Angels can help, but they can't perform the sort of life transformation the Master Path Angel did with me on their own because of the 'ripple effect'. If you imagine how it would be to try and change the life of one person without disrupting life for someone else, you'll see how complicated some of the scenarios the angels face are. There's an inevitable 'knock-on' effect that follows change of any sort, and everything has to be fitted together over time like a giant cosmic jigsaw puzzle, so real-life change requires an angel with immense power, greater than that of Guardian Angels. That's also why working with angels requires patience – you have to give them time to fit it all together – but more about that later.

Guardian Angel Names
Guardian Angels tend to have individual names and I'm listing here some examples of the wonderful names people have discovered for their angels, together with the meanings I've been able to channel for each name.

- Allambee – a quiet resting-place

- Anwar – the bright one

- Barega – the wind

- Chizoba – brings God's protection

- Harana – understanding one

- Jannia – wielder of the healing sword

- Killara – always there

- Kishmee – beloved teacher

- Maka – small fire

- Saidi – the helper

- Salina – the known one

- Solane – brave-hearted

- Zahir – shining one

Once you've learned to connect to your Guardian, you'll be able to ask their name. It's amazing how the meaning of the name always matches what you were seeking. I'll come back to asking their names later.

MASTER PATH ANGELS

Now we come to the angels I'm going to help you connect with the most. Some people call these archangels, but I feel Master Path Angels suits them better. I believe it was one of these that spoke to me in my depression and then showed me my master path on the train. These are the highest of the angels we have the power or need to connect with. These are the beings who can grant our wishes (if our wishes are the best thing for our souls) and change the course of our lives, bringing us back to our master path so that we can achieve what we're meant to in this lifetime.

The problem is that they can only intervene in our lives if they are asked to do so. And the problem with that is that they can't normally hear us, just as we can't normally hear them. In order to connect with them we have to raise our vibrations to their dimension, and that's what I'm going to teach you to do later on in this book.

Unlike Guardian Angels, you don't have one specific Master Path Angel assigned to you, and when you do connect with Master Path Angels, you won't always talk to the same angel. Different Master Path Angels take action at different times, depending on what area of life the action involves.

These angels can sometimes be seen, as in Jan's case, and something else I've noticed about them is that they seem to share a name in groups. In other words there seems to be more than one Michael, for instance, more than one Gabriel. This is still unexplained as I write, but I feel these angels can divide into several angelic beings all sharing the same character. It makes sense when you think about it, otherwise there wouldn't be enough of them to go round.

SPIRIT GUIDES

One of the questions I'm often asked is: 'How do angels differ from spirit guides?' To put it simply, an angel is a supernatural being and has always been so, whereas a spirit guide is a mortal who has died and has decided to remain in spirit on the Earth plane (as opposed to reincarnating or moving on) in order to help a particular person.

We all have spirit guides. Your guide may be someone who cared about you in a past life, or a relative in this life who has died and wants to stay with you and advise you, or a very altruistic soul who just wants to help others. Sometimes this can be because when they were alive they didn't do all they could have done in that respect and now they want to make amends.

In any event, spirit guides don't appear to have any supernatural powers to change the course of a person's life. They are very helpful, though, because, being old souls who have lived many times, they have a lot of knowledge of the human condition, which of course angels can never have because they've never been human.

What spirit guides can do is supply a little inner voice of reason when you're about to make a mistake, be of comfort to you when you feel alone and sometimes bring you reminders from your past lives or messages from loved ones who have passed over. This is the reason why a great many mediums work through a spirit guide. It seems that the guide works as a kind of transformer, providing a link between the physical and the spirit worlds.

WHAT DO ANGELS LOOK LIKE?

Spirit guides usually appear in the same form that they took on in life, but what do angels look like? The quick answer to this is, whatever you want them to look like. In other words, if you've always thought of angels as heavenly beings with gorgeous white wings and flowing gowns, then that's how they will appear to you. Or they might choose to appear in any way that seems to fit the circumstances and that you might readily accept. In reality they are beings of pure energy, so they're not constrained to any shape, size or form. I even knew of one child who saw an angel as a winged unicorn, which seemed very appropriate.

Another person I know was saved from drowning in the sea by a very ordinary-looking man. He suddenly reached down from the top of the seawall and pulled her to safety, only to then disappear in an impossible manner, as there was nowhere he could have concealed himself, and the feeling is that he was an angel.

I once had a very strange experience with what appeared to be an elderly lady. It was near the beginning of my angelic endeavours and I was completely fooled by her at first. I was alone at home that day in our rural bungalow. There weren't many buses in the area and so when I glanced out of the kitchen window while washing up, I was quite surprised to see a lady standing at the front door. I hadn't seen her coming down the front path, and visitors of any kind, without prior notice, were rare.

This lady also looked quite unsuited to long treks down country lanes, but there she was on the doorstep.

I opened the door and she told me she was in the village looking for a certain person. I offered to look in the phone book to see if I could direct her to their home, and she was very grateful, so much so that I felt compelled to invite the poor old dear inside for a drink.

I was very puzzled as to why she'd come all that way without a full address, and also dismayed that anyone would leave an elderly lady to make her own way to them. I found the person listed and we sat down with a cup of tea. At the time we only had one car, which Tony had taken to work, so I couldn't offer to drive her. I explained that where she wanted to go was quite a trek, and mostly uphill, but she seemed unconcerned. Once she was rested she seemed determined to continue on her journey, and wouldn't hear of it when I suggested walking with her. I didn't press the issue – some elderly people can get very upset if their independence is questioned. I showed her out the door and she started walking slowly up the path.

I shut the door and stepped sideways to the window above the sink to keep an eye on her progress, but she wasn't there. No one was there. Puzzled, I went to the door and looked up and down the lane. There was no one to be seen.

I don't think this was a test of my character as such. I think it was more an example to me of how diverse angels can be.

As well as this angel in the form of an elderly lady, I've seen the golden energy being I described previously, which may be close to angels' natural appearance, and I've also seen a very handsome blue-tinged winged angel in the form of a very attractive black-haired man with piercing blue eyes. This happened on a plane, and now I come to think of it, it's a bit strange that one of my major angelic events happened on a train and one on a plane. Perhaps this is a sign that I am on a spiritual journey and that the journey is more important than the destination.

As I've said, I've been a lifelong phobic when it comes to flying, and so when I found myself on a plane that seemed to be in imminent danger of crashing, I naturally was terrified almost to the point of hysteria. I'd always dreaded that if I got on a plane it would crash or that I'd become so scared that I'd be one of those people who start screaming and trying to open the door to get off! To my horror, it seemed likely that it was going to happen. The plane in question was diving around the night sky in the midst of a violent thunderstorm and storm-force winds. I was on the verge of hysteria, but the blue-tinged angel came and assured me he was holding up the plane and that it could not crash. In fact he appeared three times in all and was getting a little bit impatient with me by the third occasion. At that point I finally relaxed. No amount of pills or hypnotic therapy could have achieved what that angel achieved – peace and tranquillity in the face of what to me was real lethal danger.

That angel was in almost human form, but angels can appear as burning bushes, as animals, commonly as white buffalos, white wolves or white dogs, as beautiful butterflies and/or birds, normally in flocks of an unusually large size. They can appear as children, and as men and women of all ages. They can appear as warriors and as peacemakers. Whatever you will accept or understand the best is how they will appear. So you really can't tell by appearances.

Here's an example of the different ways in which angels can appear from Jayne, from Fleet in the UK:

I've believed in angels for many years and although I have many books on them I always feel when I read them that I have some knowledge about angels anyway, just through my intuition. I've introduced my beliefs to many of my friends when they've been at a low point in their lives. Some just laugh, but many now share my faith in the existence of angels. It's a pure joy when I feel my angels with me and I've called upon them many times when I've needed guidance.

Last year my husband was diagnosed with leukaemia and when he was in isolation in hospital for seven months before he finally had a bone-marrow transplant, I used to speak to him every night on the phone. I'd always finish our conversation with, 'I'm asking the angels to watch over you,' and then before I went to sleep I'd call them in again to remind them, particularly on the occasions when he was suffering the horrid after-effects of chemo.

One day, when I was feeling terribly unhappy about the situation, I took my dog for a long walk across the fields. My husband was having one of his bad days and I began to have a few doubts about whether the angels really were answering my prayers.

For some unknown reason I turned and looked behind me on the pathway, and two figures appeared and walked on either side of me. It was at that moment that I realized they were dressed identically in blue cloaks and had greying hair. They didn't look how I would have envisaged angels to look, but I felt sure they were angels. The strangest thing was that I realized they were twins and then I knew intuitively that they had come to assure me that they were looking after my wonderful husband.

That night I had a vision of one twin sitting at the head of my husband's hospital bed and the other at the foot. They had covered him over with the two blue cloaks I had seen them wearing. This vision went on for weeks, every night, and I took great comfort from it.

Several months later, as my husband began to respond to treatment, I realized I had stopped having the vision. The angels had gone. I think they had done what I had asked of them and that's why it was time for them to leave. I felt a bit sad that I wouldn't see them again, but they had given me hope and reassurance and I will never ever forget that.

My husband continues to recover and I still converse with angels every day. If only people would reach out more and

> *invite them in in times of need then perhaps the world would be a better place.*

These two angels were interesting, partly because of how they were dressed and partly because they were twins. The blue cloaks could have been a sign that they were healers. If Jayne had been a Cathar in a past life, the angels might have thought she'd accept the blue cloaks, because that's what they wore back then. Cathars also believed in love having power over all – another reason why the angels might have appeared in that way. Then there's the 'twin' aspect. I suspect that Jayne and her husband are twin souls, two people destined to be together. The twin aspect would therefore have been symbolism created so that Jayne wouldn't fear the vision but would understand its significance.

Are Angels Male or Female?

This is interesting because whenever people picture their Guardian Angel, they tend to picture a handsome young male warrior type, so that if they do see one, that's usually what they get. However, one of the gifts I was given by the Master Path Angel that appeared to me is the ability to create unique images of a person's specific angel. I call these Mirror Angels, because they reflect the person's soul, showing their true appearance rather than their physical one. Almost without exception, whether the subject is male or female, the angel that comes through in these portraits is female. This is probably because the questions that accompany the requests for such a reading are often of the kind where female empathy will seem more appropriate than male. So once again it seems that angels are able to adapt their appearance to suit the situation and our expectations.

Angels as Orbs in Photographs

Sometimes angels aren't visible to the naked eye but their presence is signified by an orb or other light effect in a photo. They are appearing more and more in this form now because it's an easy low-energy way of showing themselves to people who need convincing. But of course some orbs are really just dust or water droplets on the camera lens and some light effects are just tricks of the sunshine or flash photography. So how can you tell if you've captured an angel on film?

Here are the signs that tell you that an orb photo might be something special:

- One lone orb. It seems that the more orbs there are, the more likely they are to be dust or water.

- Orbs that seem to be moving or to progress or grow from shot to shot. Dust doesn't do that in a way that can be captured.

- Brightly coloured orbs. Orbs caused by dust and water are usually just off-white.

- Orbs that are partially hidden behind another object. Obviously if the orbs are dust on the camera they will be right on the lens, so it wouldn't be possible for them to be partially hidden by another object.

- Odd-shaped orbs or orbs with a part missing or chopped off. Natural particles usually have symmetrical shapes.

- Orbs that have faces or shapes within them.

- Orbs that have circles within them, arranged geometrically, a bit like crop circles.

- Very bright white orbs, as this shows high energy and is not normal for dust particles.

- Orbs that have a corona of brighter light, as again this is not normal for dust particles and shows high energy.

- Orbs that are photographed when other odd happenings are taking place, such as ornaments moving. This indicates a series of signs and should be taken as an attempt at communication.

HOW DO YOU KNOW IF AN ANGEL IS THERE?
If angels appear in so many ways, how do you know for sure if you've had an angelic encounter?

As I've tried to explain before, when in the presence of a Master Path Angel, the key is in the emotions. The love I felt the day I met one was so powerful that I've never forgotten it, and any time I remember that feeling, I *know* all over again. So, really, with Master Path Angels, you'll know without a doubt if one comes calling. It may happen during a meditation or while you're totally awake and is often heralded by a thunderclap of gigantic wings, or the sound of bells or music, or a wonderful and powerful scent. These 'special effects' are not necessary, I'm sure, but are just part of the angel giving us what we expect from a heavenly being.

Guardian Angels are a little more subtle when they appear. A classic example of one being nearby is when you're driving along a road and you suddenly *know* that there's danger ahead, so much so that you slow down and so avoid an accident. Or you might actually be involved in an accident and yet miraculously your car spins out of the danger zone. A Guardian Angel might cause you to be late leaving the house, perhaps by means of 'losing' something that can't be found and then is suddenly there in plain sight where you have looked several times before, and later you'll discover that you missed a serious accident by being two minutes behind schedule.

Shoves and Pushes

Many people have told me about being given a 'shove' that has pushed them out of danger when there was no one nearby. Kirk, from Birmingham in the UK, told me this story:

I was walking home late one night, a little tipsy, I admit. I had to cross a wide road junction made up of several different carriageways and road directions. I crossed where I could and walked along an exit lane where people weren't really supposed to walk. I found myself walking along a very narrow pavement, only about 18 inches wide, against the oncoming traffic. To my right was the high curving wall that held the bank back. I could have turned back – should have, but you know how it is, you just tend to think you can't be bothered and carry on.

I didn't think the drink had affected my balance too much, but suddenly I felt myself tipping sideways into the road. I just knew my days – minutes – were numbered at that point, because the traffic was non-stop, fast and literally inches away.

Suddenly someone shoved me backwards so hard that I swayed back out of danger and came up hard against the retaining wall of the road. There was no one else there, though.

Once I'd recovered from what I'm sure was angelic intervention, I walked carefully sideways along the path, clinging to the wall as if I was 100 feet up in the air. I might not have been given a second chance!

Terry, from Manchester in the UK, had another story to tell of divine intervention:

This happened one Friday evening after I'd got drunk with a group of friends. I was pretty 'out of it', sort of knowing what was going on but not really having any common sense about anything. I felt invincible, I guess, a bit like Superman. In those days I did tend to go too far. I ended up at the train station waiting to get a train the couple of miles home. No one else was waiting on my platform, so after a while I thought I'd just walk home along the tracks and not bother waiting for a train. The tracks went right behind my house, so I knew I couldn't get lost, and that was the only worry I had. The thought of a train coming along never crossed my mind.

I jumped down and immediately some girls on the other platform started screaming at me to get back up. I turned and was immediately blinded by the headlights of an oncoming train. Then it was me who screamed. My legs weren't working too well and there was no way I could get to safety.

Right then a man landed beside me on the tracks. I had no idea where he'd come from because there hadn't been anyone else on my platform seconds before. Suddenly everything went into slow motion and there was near silence, like when your ears have popped and everything sounds fuzzy and far away. I could still see the train coming, but it had slowed down and I felt that I was walking through quicksand.

Then the man grabbed me and I felt myself rising up. Suddenly all the noise and movement roared back into the station and I found myself swaying on the platform as the non-stop train shot past inches away from me.

There was no sign of the man and I felt like crying. He had to have been hit. He'd jumped down to save me and he'd been killed. I felt sick as I watched the train fly by, unable to snatch my eyes away, waiting for the inevitable sight of the blood and gore, and knowing that my life had been saved but also ruined by that reckless stranger's courageous act. How would I live with the guilt?

My breath was sobbing in my throat as the train cleared the station. And then I couldn't believe it – there was nothing there! The clean rails sparkled in the station lights with not a bloodstain in sight. The girls were still standing on the other platform, staring at me in disbelief. I ran for the bridge. I had to ask them what they'd seen. But by then their train pulled in and by the time my drunk and shocked legs had carried me over the bridge it was too late – they'd gone.

There was only one explanation as far as I was concerned: I had been saved by my Guardian Angel. I stopped getting drunk after that day, and maybe, just maybe, that was what it was all about.

Hugs

As well as saving you from disaster, sometimes your Guardian Angel will enfold you in their soft wings at a difficult time, such as when you're remembering a lost loved one or facing trauma of some kind. Casey, from Iowa in the USA, told me how her angel did just that for her:

I was at my son's funeral and it was the worst day of my life. He was only 28 years old when he died suddenly of a brain aneurism. I always blamed myself, as every mom would do. He hadn't answered his phone on the day that he'd died and I had worried, but hadn't taken any action. He'd told me off so many times for being over-protective, so I'd given myself a good talking-to and left him alone. Of course the medics told me that it wouldn't have made a difference, that there was nothing anyone could have done, but still I wondered.

So, I stood at the open grave and watched as they lowered my darling son's body into the cold ground. Any mother can understand what I was going through. I just wanted him back. I wanted him warm and alive. My knees felt weak and I honestly thought for a moment that I was going to fall into the hole. My husband, Barney, grabbed me and held me up.

I found myself thinking of something my son had said to me one day. He was quite religious and he believed that we all had a Guardian Angel. I had wanted so much to believe but I hadn't been able to at the time. My son had said, 'One day, Mom, when you really need it, your angel will give you a hug and then you'll believe.' So, as Barney held me I started saying to my angel in my mind, 'If you are real, then give me that hug right now. I'm ready to believe.'

Right at the very second I felt something fold around both me and my husband. It was warm and soft, and when Barney and I exchanged notes later, we both agreed it felt more than anything like a pair of wings. The feeling was so real that we both leaned into the support we got from the hugging. Other people at the service said they saw a bright white light surrounding us.

From that moment I knew my son was right, and I took a lot of comfort from that. During the next five years or so, as grief slowly softened to a quiet pain deep in my heart, I often thought of those wings in the darkest moments.

Synchronicity

As well as appearing themselves, Guardian Angels have been known to manipulate signs and things like car number plates or tunes on the radio to bring through messages. You might see the same sequence of numbers or letters at the same time of day for several days, for instance. Or, when you're on a journey somewhere, you'll see a sequence of signs on hoardings or trucks that make sense as a continuous message. These things are classic signs of angelic communication. As are finding yourself in the right place at the right time to meet someone, or being late and realizing that a beneficial series of events or a serendipitous meeting wouldn't have happened without your tardiness.

These things are known as 'synchronicity'. What does that word mean? It means that there is no such thing as a coincidence and every 'strange' little incident should be valued as a sign from your Guardian Angel. If you suddenly bump into an old friend, colleague or business acquaintance you haven't seen for a while, for instance, the chances are that it means something. Either they will tell you something you need to know or introduce you to someone you need to meet or even change your life themselves! If you are about to call an old friend and they call you right at that moment, listen very closely, because your Guardian Angel has something to tell you. Suppose you've had a song in your head all day and your partner walks into the house singing the same song. Have a good look at the lyrics, because they may have a message for you. You should always pay attention to things that could be dismissed as meaningless coincidences, because there is no such thing, and anything that looks meaningless has been placed there through the mystical power of synchronicity.

Suppose you're driving down the road thinking about making a new business deal and you're not sure if it's a good idea or not and the car in front of you has a number plate that reads 'BIG 123D'. This could be interpreted as 'Big ... Deal – it's as easy as 1, 2, 3.' The thing about synchronistic signs is that they nearly always come in threes, so later in the day a hoarding that you had never seen before might jump out at you, saying, 'Today's the day to take a chance...' Later still you might see a newspaper headline saying: '2,000 new businesses forecast this year.' All of these things could just be ignored, but a follower of synchronicity will smile and say thank you to their angel and they'll sign the contract.

Feathers

Some people swear that their angels signify their presence by leaving feathers strewn about. This used to work for me but I admit it doesn't so well now as there are so many birds where I live that I'm doubtful, but there's no doubt that when people find a feather in an unusual place, it can be the sign that they've been visited by an angel.

Dani, from Edinburgh in Scotland, told me her story of feathers:

> *I had tucked my little girl, Eden, into bed that night at about 8 p.m. At only three years old, she was my world. This was partly because her dad, my husband Alan, had died very young in a car crash when Eden was only a few days old. It had almost destroyed me, but I'd rallied just because I had Eden to take care of. She only had me too, as I had no family left alive.*
>
> *The night was cold and frosty and I snuggled up in a blanket to watch TV. I fell asleep in front of it, something I'd often done since I'd been alone.*
>
> *It was about 2.20 a.m. when I was shaken awake by the house rattling and a terrible crashing sound. Everything vibrated for a while and then slowly fell silent. I got up and ran to Eden's room, to be met by my worst nightmare. A milk tanker had skidded on the ice and crashed into my house. Eden's bedroom was just gone, entirely gone. The wall had collapsed into the room and my little girl's bed was covered in bricks. The front*

wheels of the tanker were spinning in the air a couple of feet above the rubble, as the body of the cab rested on the remains of the wall.

Screaming, I dived towards where Eden's bed had been. All I could think of was that now I'd lost everything. I clawed at the rubble and then saw a circular hole in it. I reached inside and I could feel my baby grabbing my hands. I pulled her out and tears poured from my eyes so much that I could hardly see, because Eden was untouched. She didn't have a scratch on her.

That was amazing and wonderful enough to make it the best moment of my life, but there was more. As I pulled my baby free, white feathers filled the air around her. It seemed they had been packed around her, because the hole I'd pulled her from was full of them...

Now that *was* an unusual occurrence of feathers!

Signs and Voices

You can actually 'train' your angel to show itself by something of your choice – a rose petal, a certain fragrance, a word repeated in several songs on the radio. After a time you'll develop a sixth sense for these signs in the same way that when you buy a certain make of car you instantly start seeing them everywhere. So, perhaps it's you being 'trained' rather than your angel!

You might also hear the voice of an angel. Jackie, from Yeovil in the UK, told me her angel voice story:

We were driving home late one night. My hubby, Stewart, was driving our Volvo estate, because I couldn't stand the bright oncoming headlights and tended to drive like a frightened rabbit in the dark, clinging to the edge of the road, which I could barely see. The radio was playing country music songs and in hindsight maybe heavy metal would have helped us more! I tried and tried to stay awake but I kept drifting. Every time I prised my eyes open Stewart looked wide awake and happy, so eventually I gave in and fell asleep.

I don't know how long I slept along the A303, but suddenly a voice literally screamed in my ear, 'Wake up!' My eyes shot open to see Stewart slumped in his seat, head back, and the car heading straight for a concrete bridge support on the wrong side of the road.

It was my turn to scream then. Stewart woke up, grabbed the wheel and the car just cleared the pillar! It was doubly lucky that there had been no other vehicles to crash into us as we'd veered across the wrong side of the road.

Jordan, from Sandown in the UK, told me her story, which involved angels saving her in another way:

When we were visiting the USA we were unfortunate enough to get caught up in a store robbery. We couldn't believe it when we talked about it afterwards. There we were, thousands of miles away from home on holiday, and we really were in the wrong place at the wrong time.

Three men wearing rubber masks rushed into the store and grabbed my dad, shoving him onto the floor. I was terrified and tried to go to him, but they made me lie down too.

The next thing I knew there were sirens going off. I was even more scared by then because of course American cops have guns and I thought we'd get caught in the crossfire.

It didn't quite happen that way. One of the gunmen pulled me to my feet and I knew I was going to be used as a hostage. He stood me up against the wall and yelled to the cops that he'd kill me if they didn't let him go. Of course they wouldn't do it, and I almost passed out when he pointed the gun at me and I could see the hammer rising up, just as I'd seen on TV, only this was real and I was about to be shot. I could hear my dad yelling, but my whole world had shrunk to the gun barrel. I thought I could see the bullet coming out, and then it did. I was dead, no question.

Then suddenly I felt a pressure building around me. It pushed me against the wall. At first I thought I'd been shot, but I hadn't. The pressure got harder and I felt squashed, crushed. Then there was a pop and the man with the gun was lying on the floor, bleeding. He wasn't dead, just wounded in the neck.

The police told me later that the bullet had ricocheted from something behind me and a chance in a million meant that it had hit the man. I don't believe that for a second, and neither does my dad, who says I was surrounded by white light when the gun went off and it was so bright he *couldn't keep looking at it. We both know that for whatever reason I had angels around me.*

Visits from the Spirits of Loved Ones

Under special circumstances angels can also bring the spirit of a loved one back to this world for a brief visit. I mention this one because people sometimes worry that if they see the spirit of a loved one it means they're stuck on the Earth plane and haven't moved on. But it's clear to me that when it happens, as it does in this beautiful account from Mary, of New York, the spirit has been brought through by an angel to comfort someone who is suffering greatly through their loss. This is a very important part of a Guardian Angel's duty and I'm sure one they love to do.

Mary tells her story:

My father passed away on August 27, 1967, in Spencer, New York, and was buried in Evergreen Cemetery the day before my nineteenth birthday. I'd just graduated from business school in Syracuse, NY, two weeks before. I'd had an apartment all lined up to share with several of my house-mates; I'd had an interview for a good job at Syracuse Medical Center all set up. My life was just beginning. Then Dad told me he wanted me to come home because my mother needed me. I adored my father, so his wish was my command, even though I could not understand his request.

My mother and I didn't see eye to eye very well (she had always been extremely controlling) and I just didn't see her needing me, but I did as my father asked. I got my very first job at Cornell University working in the Equine Research facility, which was just being built. I'd been there a week when my father passed away, leaving me to cope with our farm, my mother, my new job, and the insanity of it all. I finally understood why he'd said my mother needed me.

During the next nine months, I sold off the farm animals and most of the farm equipment. My mother had major surgery, followed by a nervous breakdown. I managed to hang on to my job and I grieved the loss of my father. I could hardly bear to go through each day without his strength and his support. I missed him horribly, and because of his death, my life changed 180 per cent. I had to grow up fast. I became the person on whom my mother depended to keep her world straight up. She went back to being the control freak and I hated it. It had all happened so quickly – in the flash of an eye.

One day in the spring of 1968, I was standing at the window at the top of the staircase looking out across the back yard at the empty barns and the unplanted gardens, crying, still mourning the loss of my father. Suddenly, he appeared to me in 3-D. He was wearing his coveralls and his boots and was walking across the back yard toward the cow barn. My collie dog Smokey (also deceased) was walking along beside him just as he had done when he was alive and I wasn't around.

My dad got directly across from the open window and stopped. He looked up at me and smiled, looking directly into my eyes. Then he turned and continued on toward the barn, he and my dog fading into the daylight.

I was stunned. Then suddenly I felt a sense of peace and comfort rush through my body while a warm feeling of love flushed from my head to my toes, like the buzz from a gentle electrical current. It was euphoric. [At this moment I believe Mary felt her Guardian Angel reassuring her.]

Then it all went away as quickly as it had come. In its stead, it left a sensation, a feeling, a 'knowledge' if you will, that my father was happy where he was and that I should stop grieving for him. From that day forward, I knew he was only a heartbeat away from me, that he would always be with me, and that my life would be just fine.

My dad and my angels have been with me all of my life. My father came back to escort my mother home in January 2005. One day I will see them both again.

Graham, of Norwich in the UK, told me about the time his mum came to visit after she'd died:

I had a bad back, so one evening a spiritual healer came to my house to work on it for me. We were in the dining room and I was sitting at the table with the chair round the wrong way and my head on my hands on the back of it. With me being so relaxed and the healer tuning in the way he was, some amazing energy was building up and I think that must have allowed my angel to come through with a very special gift for me, because suddenly the room was empty, the table and chairs and the healer were all gone, and I was standing up.

Then the French windows opened and my mother, who had passed away previously, walked in. She came across the room towards me, held out her arms and embraced me and then her eyes met mine as if to say, 'Everything is all right.'

It was so real and vivid. We hugged and then, as quickly as she had come, she was gone and the room was back to normal, with my friend totally unaware of what had happened. It was such a wonderful experience that I will never forget it.

Near-Death Experiences

When a person dies before their time and then returns to their body to complete their life, this is known as a 'near-death experience', or NDE, and angels sometimes feature in them. Most commonly they meet the person as they pass over and then help them to return to their body, explaining that it is not their time to die.

Seeing an angel this way and being so close to them often makes a person not want to return to the Earth plane. I have known people who were grief-stricken at having to leave the angel and come back to their bodies.

Rev. Juliet Nightingale, from Boston in the USA, shared one such emotional time with me:

In the mid 70s I was lying in a hospital bed, dying from colon cancer. My life was just ebbing away. I was bedridden for the most part, but could sometimes manage to sit up for short periods.

Being the contemplative that I was, I was always listening and observing, taking things in and trying to understand the deeper wisdom behind what was happening to me and where all of this was leading. As a result, I became more withdrawn and detached and my awareness of otherworldly things was heightened. I was entering what I later came to refer to as the 'twilight' stage. In this state, everything was altered. I got to a point where my consciousness was already making the transition from one realm to the other and I was becoming aware of other realities in other dimensions, even though I was still somewhat conscious on the physical plane.

I finally lapsed into a coma on Boxing Day, December 26, and, ironically, was declared 'dead' on my birthday, February 2! My transition was gradual as a result of having a terminal disease, as opposed to a sudden one incurred from an accident, heart attack, etc.

I became aware of a 'Being of Light' enveloping me. Everything was stunningly beautiful, so vibrant and luminous and so full of life – yes, life! I was totally and completely enveloped in divine Love. It was unconditional love in the truest sense of the word and I was never alone. Consequently, there was no sense of fear whatsoever. I was just watching the Light whirl all round me, pulsating and dancing, mak-

ing whooshing sounds, being playful at times and then very serious at other times. The colors were so beautiful.

After what I can only describe as being taken on a 'guided tour', I was asked to 'help' or 'assist' in some way in creating and determining the outcome of certain events, situations or even things affecting others. Me? Just little me? 'Oh my,' I thought. 'That's a grave and serious responsibility.' I felt so honored and so humble.

As the mood seemed to shift, I felt as if something serious was just about to befall me. I was now being told that I was going to have to return to the alien (physical) world I'd left behind – that I was needed there for something very special and significant. I needed to go back to share what had just happened to me and to let others know that life was, indeed, eternal and that death was an illusion. On a personal level, I was told that I needed to experience great love and joy in that world and finally I would be able to return home.

To say that my heart sank would be an understatement. The very thought of leaving this sacred realm where I was in constant communion with the Light and other beings crushed me in ways I could never describe. I knew how dark and foreboding that strange, illusory world that I was being asked to return to was, and it is, indeed, a world I've never identified with! However, I was, once again, reassured that the Light and other loving beings would be with me at all times and was told to remember that I'd never be alone. Gratefully – there was still no sense of fear, only *sorrow now – I realized that I had to honor the divine will that was making this request of me.*

As I reluctantly accepted this mission, I suddenly beheld before me a most beautiful being pouring tremendous love into me and filling me to overflowing. It was as if this was my gift for accepting the painful request to leave my home on the other side and return to a world that was so alien to me. This being loved me very deeply and stayed with me as I returned, continuing to radiate love and sound, and it was made clear that he would be with me always.

Astral Travel

Sometimes an angel will take a person astral travelling to stop something bad happening to someone they love. Georgie, from Wales, told me what happened to her ten years ago. She has never forgotten it and neither has her sister!

I'd been able to communicate with angels for a while and they'd often helped me with small things, but when I went to sleep on New Year's Eve in 1999 I had no idea that they were going to help me so much.

I'd gone to bed late, as you do on that night, but I'd been meditating every night and I didn't want to miss it, so I closed my eyes and began my deep breathing. The next thing I knew there was a bright presence in the room. I remember seeing the light from it bouncing off the ceiling and reflecting in the windows where there was a chink in the curtains. It enveloped me and then I found myself going up towards the ceiling. I looked down and I could see my body lying peacefully on the bed below, with its eyes shut. I was a bit scared, but the presence told me, 'You are safe. You are needed.'

We went up through the roof and into the night sky. We soared over rooftops and I remember looking down in amazement at fireworks that were still going off here and there. I even wondered what might happen if a rocket hit me. I asked myself if I was dreaming and decided that if I was it was a pretty nice dream so why worry, but really I knew enough to realize that I was astral travelling, that I had left my physical body and was travelling in my etheric one.

I started to realize that we were near where my sister Gracie and Mum and Dad lived. They didn't live together, just close to each other. Gracie had a studio flat about half a mile from Mum and Dad's house. It was a biggish town and there were lots of people still wandering around. It wasn't long before I suspected I was being taken to Gracie's flat, but I couldn't think why that would be.

Suddenly we were there. We swooped over her rooftop and then just as suddenly we were in the flat. I just couldn't believe what I saw there: Gracie passed out on the bed. She was of course drunk and totally out of it. She didn't often drink a lot, but when she did she tended to go the whole way. Mum and Dad were always on at her about it. The worst thing was she'd passed out with a cigarette in her hand and to my horror it had fallen off the bed and onto a pile of magazines, which were starting to smoulder. I could see the smoke curling up from them.

I had always worried about Gracie. It was hard to see her going the way she was without trying to stop her, but I hadn't been able to. I wanted to panic, but the being, the angel I was sure it was, spoke again. It told me not to worry. That I could save her.

Of course my first instinct was to struggle out of its grasp and stomp on the cigarette. I soon realized, though, that even if I had been able to escape, in my etheric body I wouldn't have been much use.

Then we were off again, and within about 30 seconds I was back in my body on my bed and the angel had gone. I dived on the phone, first calling the fire brigade and having to lie, saying I was in the road outside Gracie's flat and I could see flames through the window. Next I called Mum and got her and Dad out of bed. She told me later it never occurred to her in her panic to ask me how I knew Gracie was in danger. Apparently Dad left the house in his pyjamas and dressing gown at a run, and he got to the flat before the fire brigade. He had a key for emergencies (and I guess this qualified), so he was able to get in. He said the magazines were aflame, but nothing else had really caught. He was able to smother the fire with a blanket. Gracie slept right through it and also right through Dad trying to explain to the fire brigade that they weren't needed and calling me and Mum to let us know she was OK.

> *When I told Gracie what had happened, predictably she claimed not to believe me. She said I'd dreamed the whole thing up. It was just one of those weird 'sister' things. But after that I've never seen her drunk again, so I have hopes that she has changed even if she doesn't believe that her or my Guardian Angel saved her life that night.*

Your first encounter with an angel is unlikely to be as dramatic as one of these stories, although that is possible. It's more likely to be a small thing. Perhaps you'll ask for a sign and receive one, however small, such as a loved one's favourite song coming on the radio. Perhaps you'll ask for a little help and it will come from an unlikely direction. There are a million ways for an angel to enter your life. Watch and they will come!

CHAPTER 2

FOCUS PICTURES

Now you've read of some of the ways in which people have been able to connect with their angels, it's time for you to start learning how to do the same.

Some people are lucky enough to have the connection start in a dramatic way without apparently doing anything to make it happen. But even if that isn't the case with you, there are ways in which you can make a productive connection with angels.

It's time to take your road to enlightenment and a whole new you. This is the first step of many, and you have to take it and each one that follows with total belief and determination. Each step is a way of opening to angels – of starting to change your energy into a form that the higher angels can access.

At this stage, it's probably a good idea to keep your own counsel about what you are doing. Sharing ideas with people at this point can be counterproductive, because if you share the positive energy as it builds, you'll dilute it.

Also, people can be very negative about their friends and family trying new ideas, and even though those around you may mean no harm and may be genuinely concerned for you, they can still talk you down. Hug this step to yourself while you're learning. What you brood on will hatch, don't forget, and that applies to good as well as bad.

As you progress and things start to change, you'll naturally want to help your friends achieve what you're achieving. The best way to do this is to wait until you have something definite to tell them about – a small miracle, a small wish coming true, something you can hold close in the face of what may turn out to be scepticism or, worse, cynicism from them. These are emotional states that will hold you back and undo all the good you're doing. So, at first, let it be your secret.

BUILDING POSITIVE ENERGY

To get closer to angels, it's necessary to build a core of positive energy in your mind and body. There are two reasons for this.

First, negative energy can best be compared to the motion and instability of a rough ocean. If you then imagine you are like a boat adrift on that irregular sea of energy, it's easy to see how angels can find it very difficult to reach you. By creating a calm area of positivity around yourself you're creating the conditions that will allow angels to reach you and help you.

Second, a positive attitude can generate endorphins, which are nature's 'feel-good pills'. They're formed naturally in the body and are comparable to opiates, as they give you a wonderful feeling of wellbeing. It's well known that they are released during exercise, but they are also formed by positive thoughts. The wellbeing they create generates more positive feelings, which then create positive energy, and so on, establishing a never-ending positive cycle.

Not only is this beneficial in itself, but it in turn raises your vibrations. Everything on the planet has a vibrational frequency, including us. The planet itself vibrates, as does the universe, and all the other dimensions that have been discovered by physicists. The point is that you can only interact with the dimension that matches your vibrational rate. Angels exist in higher dimensions than we do, and therefore their vibrations are considerably higher than ours would naturally be. So we can only connect with the higher angels if we can raise our rate of vibration. Elevation lifts us closer to the angels' level. So by using positive energy to raise our vibrations high enough, we can cross the barrier that normally divides us from these angelic realms, and direct contact is then possible in both directions.

POSITIVE ENERGY WITH FOCUS PICTURES

A focus picture is a self-created and self-designed device that's very easy to make. It encourages positive energy, which in turn facilitates becoming closer to angels. It can be used to kick-start your progress towards angelic communication, especially if, like most people, you've found it very easy to get into an almost permanent state of negativity and are unable to find your way out of it.

The world we live in today is often heartless, totally demanding and very demoralizing. Depression is the most common illness in the world. Now while it's true that, as in my own case, deep depression can bring openness to a mind so that angels can communicate, it's much better to find a way round the problem without sinking to that low level.

So many people write to me to tell me that it seems everything in their lives has gone wrong. They'd like to pull themselves up, but they can't fight all the bad stuff that seems to be happening to them. Whichever way they turn they meet only failure, and every area of their life, from relationships to finance, is an absolute disaster. They feel cursed with bad luck and ask me, 'Why has my Guardian Angel deserted me?' or say, 'I ask and ask my angel to help me all the time, but I never get an answer.'

Of course their angel hasn't deserted them, but they can't get any answers because that sea of negativity is all around them and they're drowning in it. No Master Path Angels can hear them or reach them and all their Guardian Angel can offer is comfort and an angelic hug, which often goes unnoticed in the chaos that is their life.

People with knowledge of angels will say you have to ask or you won't get. This is true, but the problem is if angels can't hear you, because you and they can't break through the negativity, then they don't know that you're asking, so it's as bad as not asking at all.

If you are in this state, you can use a focus picture to slowly but *surely* turn your life around and bring in serious angelic help and support. This is just the first step on your new path and you shouldn't expect an instant result, but in time the results *will* come, because you are no longer focused on the negative.

Without something like this tool it's all too easy to soak up negative emotions and energy from the moment you set foot out of bed. It might only be little niggles and comments from miserable people, but it will build and build and in the end your whole being will be so drenched with negative energy that no Master Path Angel can come anywhere near you. You go back to bed in that state, sleep badly, have nightmares, wake up in a negative frame of mind and the whole thing starts all over again.

Once you're in this position everything seems to go wrong, because you're at the mercy of the universe itself. The universe is like a mirror in some respects, as it tends to reflect back exactly what's directed at it. So, if all you're able to put out is negative emotions, then negative events and outcomes are what will be reflected back at you.

What often makes things worse is that people in negative situations tend to talk endlessly about them and thereby feed and strengthen the negativity around them. They watch the news because they feel they have to keep an eye on what's going on in the world, even though they feel powerless to do anything about any of it. Then they feel worse and worse with each new atrocity or gloomy prediction that's reported, and then sit and think about it, creating an even worse scenario for themselves without even realizing that's what they're doing.

Angelic help is vital in order to have a productive, fulfilling and happy life, and that help can't come about without the negative talk, thoughts and feelings being turned into positive energy. This is step one to achieving the turnaround in your life. So how do you start?

HOW DO I MAKE A FOCUS PICTURE?

This is the fun part. In fact this 'fun' part is a very important part, because fun = positivity, and positivity = endorphins, which = yes, you're getting it, more positivity. Remember, you're trying to get off the mad world carousel and onto the Magic Roundabout. You're planting the seeds of sunflowers to take the place of the weeds.

So, take a piece of card, preferably white, and start by drawing a picture in the centre that represents the way you'd like your life to be. Any image will do – a cosy cottage in the countryside with roses round the door, a bright hummingbird with colourful wings, a smiling sun, a romantic heart, literally anything that comes to mind. You don't have to be a skilled artist – even a childish drawing will have the same effect. It's vital, though, that you take a lot of trouble over both choosing the image and drawing it. The more care and time you take over colouring and putting detail into the picture, the more it will connect with your subconscious, and the more effective it will be.

Next, write a circle of eight words or short phrases around the image. These words should also be carefully chosen and should represent the feelings you want to have in your life. Any positive words will be fine – 'happy', 'joyful', 'relaxing', 'peaceful', 'angelic', 'flight', etc. Choose whatever you would like to experience in your life.

For instance, when I did mine, I used the image of a kite flying free in the sky and the words I used were 'freedom', 'fly', 'no fear', 'blue skies', 'no clouds', 'relax', 'float' and 'magical'. When read out, they formed my personal mantra: 'I have magical freedom to fly with no fear in blue skies. There are no clouds, so I can relax and float.'

Mantras seem to happen quite naturally, even if at first the words don't appear to flow. My friend Eve used quite different words – 'joy', 'peaceful walks', 'cool forests', 'power', 'happy relationship', 'no problems' and 'independence' – but when they were put together they made this circular mantra quite easily: 'I feel joy on peaceful walks in the cool forest. I use my power to create a happy relationship with my daughter. There will be no problems and I will maintain my independence, so that I can keep the joy I feel on peaceful walks...'

HOW DO I USE IT?

Now that your focus picture is complete, all you have to do is to spend a few minutes looking at it every morning *before* you get up and before the day has a chance to imprint on you. It *has* to be *before* you get up. If you leave it, it's too late, because the first negative thought or event of your day will occur and then there'll be no going back. If you're in a negative state, even something as minor as a stubbed toe can set your negative train rolling down the line, and once it's rolling, it has no brakes, it's a real runaway.

Some people have tried to use their focus picture before going to bed, because then they have more time. This will help you sleep and not have nightmares, but it won't be of any help to you in the morning when you get up to face the day, unless you use it again then.

So, as soon as your eyes are open, stare at the drawing that you've created and concentrate on it, and it will calm your mind and help you focus on creating a good blueprint for how you want your day to be. Don't let your mind even consider the problems that are going to face you. This is not the time for them.

Say your mantra words at least eight times, concentrating on each one as well as the entire meaning. As you do so, your endorphins, those happy brain chemicals, will start to multiply and grow in your mind, and you'll start to become more and more cheerful. This will set up your energy to manifest a good day.

I have to emphasize that the reason the focus picture has to be used before you get up is so that any negative stuff that happens after that will get bounced off your positive wall, instead of being soaked up by your spirit. Once negative energy gets a foothold it's very hard to shift, and you'll be back on the downward spiral before you know it. Bad stuff will still happen, of course, but the more you use your focus picture, the more you'll find you can maintain a positive outlook despite setbacks.

There's nothing wrong with using your focus picture throughout the day either. You can use it to 'top up' your positive energy if you meet one too many miserable people to cope with. Each time something threatens your equilibrium, just bring your personal picture to mind. Bring your mantra, which you'll soon know by heart, to the front of your mind, and use it to drive bad stuff away.

Obviously, in the near future you'll still have the residue of all your old problems to deal with, so this won't bring about an instant, miraculous turnaround in your fortunes. Nevertheless, it's the first step in the right direction. As time goes by and starting off your day this way becomes habitual, your whole brain pattern will slowly change and you'll find it easier and easier to cope with the day. Even better still, as you continue to use your picture you'll find that your life will change, because your vibration will slowly but surely speed up, and this means that angels will start to hear you and be heard by you. People will start to treat you differently too, because everyone loves to bathe in the energy of a positive person. They'll want to be around you and you'll become in demand. In time, even your 'luck' will change as you attract abundance, because your positive magnetic energy will ensure that positive events and outcomes will bounce back to you from the universe. And it's all possible because you created the right energy seed in your mind from the second you opened your eyes.

You might need to use your picture and mantra every single day for at least a month to start seeing really big results, although some people do get almost instant results.

You can start asking angels for help as soon as you start using the picture, but be aware that you may need to follow all the steps in this book before the bigger good stuff starts to happen. Later I'll tell you how to ask in the best way to get results.

When this angelic device was first given to me, I tried it out with a lot of the people who were writing to me for help. I was pleased but not really surprised to hear that the angels' device worked very well and people got amazing results.

Sofia, of Cyprus, wrote to me to say:

I can't believe it! I started using the focus picture on your advice because our financial situation was really getting me down. The most worrying thing was that the water company was insisting that we owed them a huge sum of mon-

ey, which was actually owed by the previous owners of the property. Nothing we said would convince them we were innocent and we didn't know which way to turn, because there was no way we could afford a lawyer.

Four days, yes, four days after I started using the picture I'd made and asking my angels for help we had a letter saying the water company was dropping its claim, just like that!

I can't wait to see what happens next! How amazing that my angels were just waiting to help all the time and all I had to do was ask in a way that let them hear me!

Jean, of Taunton in the UK, told me:

It took a while for things to start to change for me after I started using the focus picture and the funny thing was that after each week or so I found I had to make a new picture – I suppose I was just too negative at first to do it right.

Anyway, I did start to feel a change, so I decided to ask for something – just a small thing, as I didn't want to be disappointed. I asked for a way to buy a new handbag I'd been wanting for a while but couldn't afford. This was probably after about a month or so.

That day I felt drawn to go and have a look in my garden shed. I didn't often go in there in the winter because it was right at the bottom of my 100ft garden, but I'd been told to follow 'nudges' of intuition, so I did, and I found a cat stuck in there. A chap had been taking some old wood out of the shed for his fire some days previously and he must have accidentally shut the cat in. The poor thing had obviously been in there for several days, as he'd scratched and made a mess everywhere. He was frantic to get out and was starving, so not wanting him to run off and get lost again, I put him in the kitchen and gave him some cooked chicken scraps to eat.

I left him there in the warm while I went to get some proper cat food, thinking maybe this was a new companion for me. In the shop window was a sign, and it was about the cat! I'd never noticed it the other times I'd been to the shop. The cat's owner was offering a reward for his safe return. I took him back and claimed the reward, not feeling guilty about taking it because I figured you had to accept a gift from an angel, and I bought the handbag!

As you can see, the timescale with results is variable and they can come in the strangest of ways!

A tip to use during the day if things start to weigh you down is to visualize your worries as eggs. When one of them starts to grow in your mind, visualize taking hold of it and smashing the shell into pieces. If you clutch it to you and keep it warm and cozy in the recesses of your mind, remember it will hatch!

Whatever you do, if you don't experience an angelic intervention from the focus picture alone, don't give up on getting closer to angels. Different people require different amounts of time and different devices. So, keep reading, as there are many more ways in which you can contact angels, and know that you *will* succeed.

Alternatively, you may find that using a focus picture will bring you an angel experience or such a great change in the way people perceive you that you feel you've done enough. If it does, don't stop there. Take the next step towards getting closer to angels, because the abundance they can bring you is endless.

CHAPTER 3
ANGEL CARDS

By now hopefully you've been using your focus picture consistently and so you'll be starting to feel an energy shift and new hope that things are going to get a lot better for you. Here is your next step: using angel cards. This step will also be a way of monitoring your progress, because you'll be able to see if you're getting through to your Guardian Angel with even a tiny message and whether or not they're able to reach you too. So, what are angel cards?

Angel cards are packs of cards that look a bit like normal playing cards. They come in packs, usually of about 40–50, and most New Age shops will carry a good selection of them. Each card has a stylized angel on the face, together with either one word or several words. Each pack comes with an individual set of instructions in a booklet, but in the most basic way of using them you select a card at random and the words written on it will give you your angel guidance for the day, or you ask a question and interpret the words as your answer to it.

Angel cards give your angel the opportunity to try and direct you to choose a certain card in response to a question or to reveal a word that is relevant to what your emotional state or problems are on any given day. If you use the simplest form of cards, which just have a single word on them, these words, such as 'serenity', 'faithfulness', 'truth', etc., will tell you which state you should try and concentrate on achieving during the coming day. Or you can use the ones that have a whole phrase on them and that phrase will give you some insight into your situation.

You also have the option to use the cards in a 'spread', which means pulling several cards and laying them down in a set pattern, with each card forming part of the answer to your question. The instruction booklet that comes with the cards will give you some spreads to try.

You can also adapt the spreads to suit your needs at a particular time or make up your own. For instance, you could ask about your past, present and future and then pull three cards as your answers in order, or you could ask about your mind, body and spirit and do the same thing.

CHOOSING YOUR CARDS

Anything that focuses the mind is a very useful tool in connecting with angels, and angel cards are no exception. The key is to find the cards that work best for you and to be persistent. Remember that with these cards you're re-educating your subconscious mind to work on a higher energetic vibration and every step on that ladder helps you get closer to the world of the angels. Even though most angel cards only require a few seconds' concentration, it all accumulates and starts to slowly bend your spirit in the right direction.

The first thing to do is to choose the cards that are right for you. There are many ways of doing this. Here are three that you might like to try.

The first is to spread out a selection of packs (still in their boxes) and pass your hands over them, at the same time asking your intuition to guide you to the right one. If you can't actually find a shop that stocks enough to give you a wide choice, write down the names of all the candidates on a piece of paper and pass your hand over that. Use your left hand because that hand's muscles are more likely to be guided by the right side of your brain – the side that governs intuition rather than logical thought. When your hand is over the one that your instinct tells you is right, you'll feel a pull or a tingling in your hand.

The second method is to use a pendulum to dowse over the packs. If you've never used one before, a pendulum is a small crystal or weight suspended by a cord or chain. It can be held over an item you want information on and the way it moves will give you 'yes' or 'no' answers to questions about that item. So, for instance, you could hold your pendulum over a deck of angel cards and ask: 'Is this card deck right for me?'

To get the answer, of course, you need to know when your pendulum is indicating 'yes' and when it is indicating 'no'. There are several ways in which a pendulum can move. It can rotate either clockwise or anti-clockwise. It can swing in a straight line diagonally left or right. It can move from side to side or back and forth. You need to ask your pendulum to tell you which movement means 'no' and which movement means 'yes' to it.

To start, hold the cord or chain between your thumb and forefinger about three to four inches above the pendulum. Wait until it is hanging motionless and then ask it to show you the movement for 'yes'. Once that's accomplished, then do the same for 'no'. The whole time your hand must be relaxed and not rigid. In this way you'll establish your own 'code'.

The third method of choosing your angel cards is by simple aesthetics – in other words, choose the ones that appeal to you most visually. As packs differ very much in the style of their art, the choice really is very personal, so be sure and choose the one you like most, because each time you look at them your pleasure will generate more positive energy and higher vibrations, which, as you know by now, is your main goal.

Some Ideas to Help You Choose the Right Cards

I've included a few sets of cards here that have had consistently good reviews, so if you're not familiar with angel cards, these would be good ones to start off with.

Messages from Your Angels: Oracle Cards, **Doreen Virtue**

Of the many sets of cards designed by Doreen Virtue, these always top the popularity charts. People say they are very beautiful and accurate.

Debbie, from Grays in the UK, had this to say when interviewed about these cards:

> *I've used these cards for several years and in fact have just bought a new pack of the same ones. When my mum died they were a huge comfort for me and I gradually came to believe that the angels were channelling messages through from her. Without them I don't think I would have survived the terrible loss.*

Angels of Light Cards, **Diana Cooper**

Another hot choice is these cards designed by Diana Cooper. People seem to like the fact that they come in their own little storage bag and so are easy to carry around.

Alison, from Epsom in the UK, said:

> *I really needed convincing when I bought these cards, as I'd already tried really hard with Tarot cards but had been unable to link with them. I immediately resonated with these, though, and I used them all the way through several stages of a job application with successful results.*

Daily Guidance from Your Angels: Oracle Cards, **Doreen Virtue**

My third choice is another pack designed by Doreen

Virtue. People say they are simple and quick to use and offer practical day-to-day advice.

Jilly, of Doncaster in the UK, told me:

I always thought you had to be psychic to use any kind of divination cards, but I was pleasantly surprised to discover that anyone can use these. I even started giving my friends readings and to my surprise I was very accurate.

Angelic Messenger Cards: Divine Guidance for Personal Healing and Spiritual Discovery, Meredith Young-Sowers

This pack is a bit different in that it combines angels with the symbolic beauty of flowers.

Maureen, of Idaho in the USA, said:

I loved actually using these cards in the garden among the real flowers. It seemed to amplify their power. I was surprised by how uncannily accurate these cards were.

Tarot of the Angels, Lo Scarabeo

As it says, this is actually a Tarot card set inspired by angels.

Janet, of Pennsylvania in the USA, said:

With lively imagery, artist Arturo Picca displays a wide variety of angelic beings in Tarot of the Angels. From warrior angels to playful cherubs, dark entities to humble servants of humanity, a myriad of vocations and persuasions finds expression in this ethereal deck. If you're looking for an angel-themed deck that isn't airy or exclusively New Age positivism, you may want to give Tarot of the Angels a try. The imagery invites speculation and contemplative musings, as well as story possibilities, intuitive insight and spiritual comfort (and perhaps warnings?) from a host of angelic messengers.

Tarot Talismans: Invoke the Angels of the Tarot, Chic and Sandra Tabatha Cicero

According to Chic and Sandra Tabatha Cicero, the Tarot is much more than a collection of symbolic images, it's a vibrant ecosystem of interconnected energies and entities. In what they call a 'groundbreaking approach to Tarot', they show how these powerful cards can be magically transformed into talismans and amulets.

June, of Sydney, Australia, said:

This set is very good for the novice reader, but also provides a lot of new information for the advanced light-worker.

There are many sets of cards to choose from and you can trust that you'll be guided to the cards that are right for you.

HOW TO USE ANGEL CARDS

I've seen people in mind, body, spirit shops take a card on a daily basis and they seem to be happy with that, but really that's just random chance. You can't fully access your subconscious unless you prepare properly. So, the best way to use your chosen cards is as follows:

Pick a quiet time when you're unlikely to be interrupted and get a pen and paper ready to make notes on.

Take your cards out of their box, taking a moment or two to handle them and attune yourself to them. Admire the colours and designs of your cards to bring positive feelings forward.

Relax. Close your eyes and control your breathing, so that you make a better connection with your higher self and with your spiritual core.

Ask your Guardian Angel to come forward and be ready to respond to you. Open your heart and soul to your angel and visualize white energy flowing from you to them and back again.

If you have just one question in mind, ask it silently or out loud.

When you feel ready for the answer, open your eyes. Quietly and calmly, select a card and turn it over.

Now it will be down to your own intuition to interpret the card. Focus on the word or message and take a few moments to let it sink into your mind. Write down anything that comes to mind and then reflect on what you have been given and what it means to you.

If the answer turns out to be the correct one or if the card has a deep connection to your question, then you'll know that communication between you and your angel is starting.

Questions and Answers

If you want to ask a complicated question, or multiple questions, then you'll need to select a spread to find your answers. You can either follow the instructions that come with the pack to select an appropriate spread or follow your intuition and select the number and layout of cards that feel right to you. Either is fine, and the more you practise using your intuition in this way, the more quickly you'll hone your skills.

Make your questions as specific as you possibly can, and when interpreting the answers, accept everything that immediately comes to mind. A lot of people go wrong with these and any psychic readings by over-interpreting the answers they get. For instance, if the first thing that sprang to mind was 'Being of help', don't sit there trying to think what or whom it might refer to, because most times when you do this you'll come up with the wrong answer, focus on it and then miss the right opportunity when it comes along. Just accept that at some point during the coming day you'll be called upon to help someone, and stay open-minded about who, when and where. That way you'll be ready for anything and won't be caught napping.

When to Use the Cards

There are many occasions when angel cards can be useful:

- Pick a card first thing in the morning and use the message there to help sustain your positive energy (started with the focus picture) throughout the day.

- If you have a friend or family member who is ill or who is going through a rough time, pick a card for them and just spend a few moments sending them the energy of the message on the cards. You can be sure that it will be just what they need.

- If you're going for a job interview and feeling a bit nervous, or you're starting a new project or job that you're feeling anxious about, pick a card and the message there will be just what you need to keep you calm and confident.

- If you're facing a difficult or onerous task, or are scared of a trip to the dentist, pick a card and it will help steady your nerves.

- Pick a card on your birthday or wedding anniversary to give you an idea of what lies in the year ahead.

- If you've fallen out with somebody and you want to make amends but don't know how, choose a card and send the message with love and light.

If the cards don't work immediately for you, whatever you do, don't give up and decide that you don't have what it takes. If you were learning a new skill such as playing the guitar, you wouldn't expect your first chords to be perfect. Some things take time. Have faith, keep trying and it will happen. Don't try and force it. Stay calm, centre yourself and start again.

TAKING CARE OF YOUR CARDS
Keep your cards as clean, crease-free and pure as you can. After all, these are tools for talking to angels with!

It's always good if you have a soft pouch to keep them in. A nice box would be even better.

Keep some crystals with them to help cleanse them and always treat them with respect.

If they do get worn over time you should replace them, because otherwise your selection will be compromised by the bends or creases and any grit or dirt on the cards.

SHARING YOUR CARDS
Once you feel you're making progress with doing readings just for yourself and you feel your connection with angels is growing, you can start enlisting friends as guinea pigs. Now's the time to share your journey with them, because by now, even if they are sceptics, you should be able to produce some minor messages that make sense to them and so start to help them suspend their disbelief. Of course this will have a knock-on effect on you, too,

because every time you successfully connect for them, and therefore encourage them to take a step in the right direction, you'll continue with your own energy renewal and your connection with angels will strengthen.

Always start by asking your own Guardian Angel to help you bring through messages from the other person's angels. Then carry on just as you would when using the cards for yourself, except of course you'll be asking your friends' questions on their behalf and giving them your interpretation of the answers you get. You can pull the cards yourself or allow them to do so. It shouldn't make any difference to the answers.

It's perfectly OK to treat the whole thing as a bit of fun (angels like fun too), if it's necessary in order to get your friends and family to be the subject of your readings.

You will find, though, believe it or not, that it's much easier to read cards for strangers, because the biggest tendency in fledgling readers is to over-interpret what the cards tell them. The better you know the person and the more you think about the answers, the more you'll go off in the wrong direction. The golden rule is to 'say what you see' and nothing else. So have your friends think of an area of their lives that they have questions or doubts about and then pull a card, or have them pull a card, and just give them the word or words that are written there. You'll be amazed to find that it *will* make sense to them.

To show you how you might develop in time, I searched for a card-reader I felt was exceptionally good, and after a lot of research and recommendations, I found Bev Lewis, who operates a holistic and spiritual health centre in Lincolnshire called Solana.

One of her clients I spoke to was a lady called Sue, and she described the experience of her reading from start to finish. To me, this demonstrates the perfect reading and is the sort of thing you should be aiming for, both for yourself and when you do readings for others.

Sue explained:

I needed some guidance with regard to which route to go down with my business, which was virtually dead. I thought I might also have some issues relating to my marriage break-up eight years previously and to the resulting relationship with my adult children, which might have been causing blocks.

I was drawn to Doreen Virtue's Healing with the Fairies Oracle Cards, so that was the set we went with.

Bev put the following question to the fairies:

Sue feels that she may be at a crossroads or other junction and is unsure of the direction to take. Also, she has family issues which may need healing and she would like guidance and support here, please.

One card immediately jumped out of the deck while Bev was shuffling them – this was the main influence. It was the 'Family Harmony' card! I was told that my relation-

ships with family members were healing. This was a great comfort to me. This is what Bev said:

> I believe you were right in thinking that some of the issues relating to your previous relationship and the decisions of your children were impeding your manifestations in your business environment. But it seems that you must hold your vision of the intended direction for your efforts and know that they will be made manifest, and in the meantime, give your doubts and fears, family dilemmas and issues to the fairies and walk away, knowing they will bring the highest possible outcome for you. I get the distinct impression that a new birth will bring big changes to the family dynamics and be a perfect 'icebreaker'.

This last sentence in particular I found amazing, as my daughter had told me just the previous week that she was trying for a baby! I had always felt that a baby would be the bridge needed to bring her and my new partner together.

One card Bev pulled for me that she found slightly worrying was the 'Sexuality' card, but as you can see from what she says, the fairies worked hard to bring this to my attention:

> I was told to select the following three cards by dividing the deck into three and selecting the top card from each one. The funny thing was, though, I was made to put a

few more from the bottom of one third into the middle third, and that was the 'Sexuality' card needing to come forward.

It was a worry when I saw it, as it's a very personal card and I was unsure if it was appropriate to include it, but they had worked hard at bringing it forward, so I did.

I found this card very appropriate, as my partner and I did have sexual issues we needed to address, which we had both been ignoring. We spoke about it on the day of the reading and resolved to do something about it! Thank you, fairies!

Another card which jumped out was the possible/most likely outcome: 'Miracle Healing'. This is what Bev told me:

A general theme for their guidance seems to be that of positive thoughts bringing positive actions and rewards. Focus your thoughts on that which you wish to have in your life and avoid slipping into negative thought patterns or dwelling on negative situations which may hold them in place. It seems you have a very bright and prosperous future ahead of you – all you need to do is live it in a virtual environment every day to make it real!

Another 'nail on the head' here, as I have been guilty of negative thinking ever since I've had no income from my business, always thinking, 'I can't afford this, I can't do that…' My new day's resolution is: 'Think positive!'

I feel so much better for having this reading. I feel uplifted and more positive, and my heart feels lighter. I am so very grateful to Bev. Through her my angels/fairies have shown me I do have a bright future to look forward to!

Angel Cards are a very useful tool to help awaken your intuition and draw you into an energy level that will bring you closer to angel dimensions. However, don't worry if they don't seem to suit you or don't immediately give you the required effect, because there are many other tools. Each one of them is meant to be used as a focus for the mind, and in the following chapter there are many more to choose from.

CHAPTER 4
TOOLS TO ATTRACT ANGELS

As well as focus pictures and angel cards, there are other tools you can use to enhance your energy and raise your vibrations, such as singing bowls, drums and crystals. Which one will attract the particular angels that can help you?

SINGING BOWLS

Crystal singing bowls are made from pure silica sand particles, which are made of crushed quartz. The sand is dropped into a centrifugal force spinning mould, an electric arc torch is ignited in the centre of it and it is heated to several thousand degrees centigrade. The heat melds the particles of sand into a solid bowl shape comprised of a material resembling glass. These bowls come in many sizes and each size creates a different note.

Tibetan singing bowls are made of brass and are actually bells rather than bowls, but instead of being hung up they are stood on their bases and 'rung' with a stick that makes the sides vibrate, producing a sound.

All singing bowls produce a variety of sounds equivalent to notes on a scale and each one corresponds to a chakra of the body. Chakra means 'wheel' in Sanskrit and the body has several spinning energy centres that resemble spinning wheels. These energy centres, or chakras, regulate the flow of energy through our spiritual system, creating colours in our energy fields. There are seven chakras: the crown, brow (or third eye), throat, heart, solar plexus, sacral centre and root (or base).

This is how the various notes from the singing bowls correspond to the chakras:

- C: Root (or base)
- D: Sacral centre
- E: Solar plexus
- F: Heart
- G: Throat
- A: Brow (or third eye)
- B: Crown

So it makes sense to choose a bowl that will affect the energy of the part of your body that you feel is most blocked. If you're unsure, the solar plexus is always a good place to start, because the solar plexus chakra is one of the main power chakras of the body. It's also greatly associated with the functioning of the aura or psychic energy field, which is the very thing we're trying to change.

If you're still unsure, it's quite acceptable to ask in the shop to hear the tones of the bowls and to pick the one you feel most comfortable with. Hand-beaten Tibetan bowls have richer and more varied tones, but the machine-made ones are easier to play and may be better for a beginner.

How Do You Use Singing Bowls?

Crystal Bowls

Crystal bowls are played by the gentle rubbing of a stick covered with either a rubber ball or suede around the outside edge of the bowl. To play, put the bowl on a flat surface with its rubber ring in the centre to stop it sliding around. It's best to rub the bowl in an anti-clockwise direction and not too hard. It will get louder the harder and faster you circle, but it doesn't have to be loud to work.

You should play the bowl for about 15 minutes to get the full effect. You'll feel a vibration which will travel through your body, releasing blockages and clearing negative emotions. Start with the intent of drawing angels to you.

Tibetan Bowls

Tibetan brass bowls are played with a carved wooden stick. This time hold the bowl (which will usually be smaller than a crystal bowl) on the flat of your hand. Slide the playing stick around the outer edge of the bowl. The vibration will start first and then the bowl will start to sing. It's a good idea to occasionally hold the bowl up to your ear to get the full benefit of the tone.

DRUMMING

Drumming closely resembles the beating of a heart, so it's no wonder that many, many different sorts are used to raise vibrations and clear negative energy. There are Middle Eastern, Native American and Celtic drums – the choice is yours. Just choose the one that sounds best to you.

This is a more specialized instrument, so it's a good idea to join a drumming circle. Under instruction, drumming can access your ancestral depths, transcend everyday worries and take you to a spiritual place. In a room full of people drumming it will be almost impossible not to let go and live in the moment, instead of living in your worries.

SOUND THERAPY

All sound is vibration. If you can retune your body's vibration, then you should be able to meld it with the vibration of your mind and soul, creating a harmonious symphony of sound that will raise your total vibration – the ultimate aim of all these exercises.

I asked Diane Egby-Edwards, the UK's top expert in the field of sound therapy, to explain exactly how sound works on the body and how it can be used on people who normally find their minds racing too much to allow them to relax. Without the ability to relax and switch off the modern world, a higher vibration cannot be achieved. This is what she told me:

I'm a hypnotherapist and sound healer and I've found 'singing' bowls to be especially useful not only for creating altered states of mind but also as a healing medium for treating all kinds of problems.

The brain in ordinary mode has fast brainwaves. These are called 'beta' waves. When we become calmer and more relaxed, we move into 'alpha' or even 'theta' brainwaves, which are slower. These feel good and it is in these slow waves that healing can take place more effectively.

To slow our brainwaves down we mostly use various types of relaxation methods, which take a little time. However, there is another way, a much quicker way, into slow waves.

Interestingly, the brain copies its environment (which explains why so many people suffer anxiety in busy shopping centres), so when it hears the sounding of a bowl in a therapy situation it automatically copies what it hears. At first, when a bowl is sounded its frequency is fast, just like the brain in its usual state, but then as the sound begins to fade, the frequency gets slower and – guess what – the brain copies. The patient is now moving into a slower, more comfortable brain-state. So, bowls are really good for help-

ing people into altered states of consciousness very quickly, much more quickly than the more traditional ways of calming the mind.

Once the mind is 'entrained' to the sound waves coming from the bowl, a sound practitioner can use the waves to send healing into the patient. I have helped many people by using crystal, Tibetan and Japanese bowls in this way, and the effects seem magical!

A typical example was a lady who came because she was in a chronic state of anxiety. Life was a burden to her – she had no joy in living. She came believing that my treatment would not be able help her (yet part of her knew it would be successful). She had already consulted several other therapists and sadly she could see no light at the end of her tunnel. However, within moments of her putting her feet up and closing her eyes, I knew that sound would heal her. To begin I sounded a C# crystal bowl and she went into slow brainwaves beautifully. Using my pendulum, I dowsed her body and found a dense patch of negative energy lying over her right shoulder. I sounded a C# and an A Japanese bowl over that precise area. I then gave her constructive, positive suggestions that would be taken by the sound waves deep into her subconscious mind. These would play a part in her healing. During the session other bowls played their part in the process. The outcome was lovely, because from that first session she began to feel better. I saw her a couple more times and progress was sure and lasting. Her outlook on life was transformed.

> *Although sound energy has amazing potential, we are only just beginning to understand the profound effects it can have on the lives of those who seek its help.*

Although the potential of sound is just starting to be understood, it certainly seems that it can bring the mind and body into a meditative state, and at that point a higher energetic vibration can be achieved.

The key is to remember that:

Fast brainwaves = low energetic vibration = little or no angelic connection

Slow brainwaves = high energetic vibration = high probability of angelic connection

So if you would like to try sound therapy, it just might put you in touch with angels…

CRYSTALS

All the things we've concentrated on so far have only dealt with your personal energy, but of course you can be easily influenced by the cares of running a home, being the breadwinner, raising your children and trying to be yourself and find time for that person. If things aren't as harmonious as they should be, negative energy will thrive. You should be able to find a comforting and comfortable retreat from the world in your own home. However, in today's reality, this often requires some effort. The use of crystals in the home can regulate the energy and prevent arguments – i.e. negative emotions – and help you on the way to becoming a balanced person with a vibration high enough to reach your Guardian Angel.

How to Choose Crystals

Most crystal users will tell you that you don't choose them, they choose you. Many times I've watched people in New Age stores walking round the crystal section. You can almost predict the ones they're going to end up buying, because they keep being drawn over and over, back to the same ones. So if you are interested in working with crystals, just go with the flow and go where you are drawn.

Once a type of crystal has chosen you, spread several specimens out and pass your left hand over them, just as you did with the angel cards. When you feel that pull or tingle, pick the relevant crystal up and hold it gently in your hand. The right pressure is about the same as you'd use to hold a butterfly captive. Held this way, the right crystal will quickly grow warm, if not hot, in your hand, and you'll know that that's the one for you.

All crystals vibrate in a very structured way; that's why they're used in calibration machines. By allowing your intuition to help select the right crystal, you're also allowing your Guardian Angel to influence your choice. This is good, because you'll then automatically choose the one that has the vibrations that most closely match your angel's. All these things are cumulative and aid your journey.

Where Should You Place Crystals to Re-energize your Home?

Flat spots in the home, areas that seem to trigger relationship problems or arguments with children and areas that create 'deficient abilities', such as the kitchen of a terrible cook, or a master bedroom with no 'master', can be rectified by the placing of crystals in and around the building.

Crystal remedies often recommend exotic or hard-to-come-by stones, but the same results can be achieved with a simple pallet of crystals that are common and won't break the bank. They are clear quartz, rainbow quartz, rose quartz, smoky quartz, fluorite, citrine, amethyst, lapis lazuli and bloodstone.

The first thing to do is to recognize the areas that need help, both in the building and in the people who inhabit it. Wait until you have the house to yourself and then ask your angel to direct you to the negative areas. Walk all around the house and garden. Feel for any area that may have a depressed feel about it, or likewise a very disturbed and chaotic feel. There will be places where you feel you can easily sit quietly and meditate and others where you feel disturbed. A very good barometer test for your home is to hold a party for people you are drawn to. Watch carefully to see which areas they congregate in and which areas they avoid. This will give you further clues as to which rooms in your house are working well energy-wise. Once you have sorted out the home into good and bad areas, you can begin to clear the energy and make your home a place where angels will feel welcome.

For any area that feels dour and dismal, you need to place a fairly large piece of smoky quartz on the window sill. This will dissolve any negative energy in the room and also any anger and resentment that might be lurking in the corners. It's a slow-acting, long-lasting activator and will take a lot of negativity before it needs cleansing.

If you feel that any areas of your house may harbour unwanted entities in the form of ghosts or just lingering memories of traumatic incidents, then you need to place a piece of rainbow quartz in each corner as high up as possible. If there are any spirits muddying your energy with theirs, they will be able to follow the rainbows to the light. So, you will not only clear the room but also help any disembodied spirits find a way forward. These crystals will need cleansing quite often at first, but then less as the energy stabilizes.

For any areas of the house that seem to always be needing repairs and money spent on them, use pieces of citrine dotted on the surfaces. Citrine encourages wealth, so in the type of space that eats money, it will reverse the situation. It's also a balancing stone, so it will make sure that money spent will be replaced. It's also a good idea to use this crystal wherever you do your household accounts, for obvious reasons. It won't help you with the taxman, but it will help you end up in credit. Citrines rarely need cleansing.

If there's a room where there always seems to be bedlam and nobody can relax, try putting an amethyst cluster or ball on the window ledge. This will give a calming effect to the energy of the room and, because it works on the throat chakra, will help stop harsh words and arguments. The amethyst will also bring a greater feeling of contentment to those who use the room. Not only that, but it will help release any frustration felt at hard words from others outside the house during the day. If the room is constantly untidy, it will help people in it to want to smooth things and bring order to them. It will need regular cleansing.

Children's rooms can be a bit chaotic, but that's natural. What's more likely to need help is the room of a child who is stressing out about exams or being bullied. This room needs some rose quartz. This will bring a quality of self-love and self-respect to the person who uses the room most and thereby increase their confidence in themselves. The rose quartz chunks should be as big as you can afford, and they should be placed as near to the bed as possible. Tell your child they will also bring their Guardian Angel to them at night, to give them restful sleep and sweet dreams. They will need regular cleansing.

If there is a room where you go to try and meditate your cares away, you should invest in some fluorite. This incredibly beautiful multi-coloured crystal will aid you in letting go of the worries of the outside world. Even someone who has never tried meditating or has never been successful at it will find the energy of fluorite a help. If you doubt this, place a good piece of fluorite in your hand and just stare at it. Look and see the tiny worlds inside, where galaxies seem to swirl and where the colours merge, blend and divide, to gain a glimpse into another world. After a few moments, what are you thinking? The answer to this question is generally, 'Nothing.' That is the beauty of fluorite. It clears the mind of clutter. It needs occasional cleansing.

If there is somewhere you go to be creative, you should try placing some lapis lazuli around the chair you work from. It will encourage your creative juices to flow and allow your mind to expand its ideas. It can also be very useful for the place where your children study or do homework. Their marks will improve! It will prevent creative problems such as 'writer's block' and enable ideas to flow freely. It won't need much cleansing. If, however, you work at a computer or have any other electrical device in that room, then a chunk of rose quartz will help combat the negative energy flow from it.

Lapis will also work in the kitchen of a bad cook. Whilst it won't transform you overnight into Gordon Ramsay, it will help – and it won't involve swearing!

If you have a grand room available and dream of holding sparkling dinner parties, then what you need is the biggest piece of clear quartz you can find. Place it where its multi-facets catch any available light, and light a candle next to it whenever possible. When you do have a party, the quartz will encourage witty conversation and meaningful relationships with others. It will brighten wooden furniture and give the whole room an atmosphere of warmth and welcome. It will need cleansing after every party.

Finally, if your problems stem from a lack of romance in the master bedroom, place bloodstone next to the bed. This mighty stone, often used in the breastplates of high priests, will encourage the 'combatants' to be here and now rather than dwelling in the hurtful past. In this way it will prevent old grievances being aired or thrown in the faces of those who really do love each other. It will help to bring about compromise and, perhaps most important of all, will enable the talker to listen and the listener to talk. It will need cleansing every week.

Cleansing your Crystals

When you need to cleanse your crystals, the easiest, cheapest and often most effective thing is to wash them carefully. It's best to use some kind of purified water if you can, either a good mineral water or at the very least filtered water. Pat the crystals dry with some clean paper and then leave them to absorb 24 hours of sunlight and moonlight on an exposed window sill. It doesn't matter if it's cloudy – the crystals will still get the energy they need.

Useful Crystals

Listed below are some crystals that are commonly used and easily available.

- *Amazonite:* Use this to keep a cool head when all around are losing theirs! This stone helps the mind remain calm during stress, which enables you to use your intuition while under pressure.

- *Amber:* This is ideal if you are feeling depressed and will also make you attractive to happy people.

- *Amethyst:* Nightmares are banished by amethyst and negative energy is repelled, so this is a vital crystal to have around you.

- *Ametrine:* A mixture of amethyst and citrine, this helps combine the physical world with the spiritual.

- *Aventurine:* Arguments in the family should be a thing of the past with the help of this stone.

- *Azurite:* Jealousy can be combated by this crystal and it will also prevent old resentments from getting the better of you.

- *Bloodstone:* This stone gives you a wonderful feeling of protection.

- *Blue lace agate:* There is a fine line between assertion and aggression. This stone prevents you from crossing that line, but allows you to speak your mind.

- *Carnelian:* If you find yourself having to play the part of Solomon in your household, this stone will help you to be balanced and access your wisdom.

- *Celestite:* 'Peace' and 'serenity' will be the buzzwords in your house if you use this crystal.

- *Citrine:* Known as the 'cuddle stone', this will give you a feeling of having company even if everyone seems to be ignoring you.

- *Clear quartz:* A very powerful crystal. You just can't have too many of them. This is the one I find most useful of all, because it can be used for multiple purposes. This is because quartz is the only crystal that will pick up your intent and attune itself to your energy automatically. It's the absolute 'all-purpose' stone.

- *Fluorite:* The ultimate meditation stone. Lose yourself in its swirling green and purple universes.

- *Garnet:* Gives you the determination you need to achieve your goals.

- *Haematite:* This stone will give you self-confidence, but won't make you too pushy.

- *Howlite:* This stone combats nightmares and aids restful sleep.

- *Jasper:* No matter what the day has thrown at you, you will be helped to speak to angels by using this crystal.

- *Kyanite:* When your emotions are ragged and you feel you just need support, this stone will give it to you.

- *Labradorite/spectrolite:* Everyone has a 'third eye', and this stone will help you open it.

- *Lapis lazuli:* If nobody's talking to each other, watch this crystal turn them all into chatterboxes.

- *Malachite:* This stone will help you balance the spiritual with the practical.

- *Moonstone:* If your man has gone quiet but you know there's a problem, this will encourage him to share.

- *Peridot:* When your feelings have been hurt, this stone will help you keep it in perspective.

- *Rhodonite:* If your family is driving you insane, this stone will restore harmony, while leaving them in no doubt who is in charge.

- *Rose quartz:* This brings self-love, heals emotional wounds and helps overcome grief of any kind.

- *Rutilated quartz:* If you feel your personal power has been used against you, this will help restore your self-esteem and make home somewhere you feel safe.

- *Selenite:* This will help you feel connected to that great big universe out there.

- *Sodalite:* If you are over-sensitive and in danger of saying something you'll regret, use sodalite to see things clearly.

- *Smoky quartz:* This stone is very good at absorbing negativity and leaving you feeling fresh and new.

- *Tiger's eye:* Wish upon a tiger's eye if you want your dreams to become real.

- *Tourmaline:* Protects your house from negative invaders.

- *Turquoise:* Gives you what you need rather than what you want.

- *Unakite:* If the family's all down with 'flu, scatter this stone around to help soothe them. It will also help root out the cause of the illness or the problem that is making them prone to sickness.

Whatever crystals you use, change them around from day to day, because after a while they get 'full up' and need a rest.

Crystal Elixirs

These are not at all difficult to make. If you drink a few drops of them they will help cleanse your system and transform any negative energy that you soak up from negative situations during the day or any negative emotions that come from other people.

The most important part is deciding which crystal to use. Some crystals can impart lead or other noxious substances to water, which would be very dangerous. It's best to stick to anything from the quartz family or amber. Do check with the store you buy them from that your crystals will be safe to use in this way.

Once you have your chosen crystal, just drop it into a bottle of pure spring water. Make sure this is a glass bottle, not plastic. This is because you leave the elixir in the sun and moon for a day and a night, and plastic, if heated, can leave the water contaminated by chemicals.

If you use these tools diligently for a few weeks, your energy vibrations will be starting to quiver with expectation as their pulse rate accelerates. You'll know when it's time to move on to the next, most vital stage in your development, that of learning to meditate. All of the previous chapters have been designed to get you ready for this, the 'big one'. This will be when two-way communication with your angel will start to happen and you'll be able to really start to change your life. Take a deep breath and move on!

CHAPTER 5
MEDITATION

Welcome to your graduation. This step is the most important of all when it comes to getting closer to angels, and taking it should ensure your connection to angels every day for the rest of your life. It is learning to meditate.

WHAT IS MEDITATION?

Meditation in its simplest definition is a way of switching off the material world. During a successful meditation, you go 'somewhere else'. The worries of the world won't be able to touch you. You become one with your higher self – your soul. You might still be aware of the world around you, but it won't concern you. Some might call it a deep prayer state, some might call it self-hypnosis, but whatever name you give it, it's your best and brightest tool for raising your vibrations enough to reach the realms of angels. It's during meditation that you'll have the best chance of actually getting to meet a Master Path Angel.

Meditation can last for seconds and it can last for hours. Some people find it easy and some very difficult. If you've followed the steps preceding this one, then you have every chance of being well-prepared and therefore successful. And the more you practise it, the better you'll get and the deeper into the right mind state you'll go.

There are many forms of meditation. You can start with the kind that happens naturally. For instance, you might be standing at the sink washing up and your mind might start to drift. Or you might be driving the car and suddenly realize that while you've obviously negotiated the roads safely, you have no recollection of travelling the last few miles. This is quite an important example, because it proves that the conscious mind and the unconscious mind can operate independently of each other. You might naturally enter a hypnogogic state as you're falling asleep or a hypnopompic state as you're waking up and find yourself receiving strange messages and images. (A hypnogogic state is those few moments of 'half-sleep' you feel just as you're falling asleep. It's a delicious and seductive feeling in which you are totally relaxed and therefore your subconscious is open to suggestion and angelic interaction. A hypnopompic state is the reverse. This happens just before you fully awaken when you still feel the euphoric sense of all being well with your world – before any problems of the coming day spoil it. This positivity helps angels get close to you.)

After these 'natural' meditations there comes the deliberate 'everyman's' meditation, where you send yourself into a trance-like state by using concentration and the methods listed below.

You might become very enthusiastic about the experience and decide to learn one of the more esoteric methods of mediation as practised in yoga or Zen Buddhism, for instance.

Whichever method you end up using is a personal choice and once you've learned the basic principles, you'll be in a position to look further afield for the path that suits you best.

HOW DO YOU MEDITATE?
Everyman's Method
Before you start any form of meditation, state your intent. If you are using it to meet angels and develop a relationship with them, then state this by fixing the idea firmly in your mind. Also, ask your guides and Guardian Angel for their protection during your 'open' time.

> When you feel ready to start, make sure that you won't be interrupted by the phone or a knock at the door. Shut all pets into another part of the house so that they don't disturb you. Close the curtains if you prefer a darkened room and find the most comfortable place to sit or lie down. Some people prefer to sit and others to lie down, and it really doesn't matter which. Just choose the one that makes you feel most at ease.

Before you begin, close your eyes for a while and think your way right through your body, relaxing each muscle and nerve from the top of your head to the tip of your toes, making sure you don't miss any part out, including your mouth and jaw. Take your time. If any part of you is tense, it won't work. This should be an enjoyable experience from start to finish.

As you start to relax, control your breathing. Become ultra-aware of every breath you take and feel it oxygenating your body as it passes through your lungs and then spreads right through your vascular system.

See each in-breath as golden or violet light, and see each out-breath as a dark colour laden with any unease or negative emotions you have within you. Feel each breath cleanse you more and more until the out-breaths change gradually to the lighter, brighter colours.

Sink into the chair or bed that you're sitting or lying on and feel as one with it, as if it too is part of your super-relaxed body.

Breathing and Counting

This is the simplest method of meditation. It works well whether you have a short or long time available, but when you first try it you might find it takes you many attempts before you succeed. It also works well when you're about to go to sleep. If you do it then, it enhances the hypnogogic state and you're more likely to experience messages from your angel as you drop off.

Start from 200 and simply count your breaths backwards, one for each number. The reason you are counting backwards is to make your mind concentrate a little harder. If you find your mind switching over to making a shopping list or something similar, then don't feel frustrated, just start again at the beginning.

Once this meditation works, you'll suddenly find yourself somewhere else, or you'll hear a voice inside your head that isn't your own, or you'll see an image of something. What usually happens at that point is that you're so excited to have 'made it' somewhere that you snap out of it instantly. If that happens to you, don't worry, just start over. This is all about training your mind and it takes time.

Once you do get the hang of it and can reliably switch off your conscious mind and switch on your subconscious mind, you'll be able to start understanding the words, visions and places that you see. You'll start to be able to control the process and link in with angels.

This sort of mediation doesn't always initiate long and meaningful conversations with angels, but it's a very good way to get messages and start to understand how meditation works.

Visualization
This type of meditation can be very effective and will enable you to meet angels and have deep communion with them. During it you may be taken to your past lives,

or your future, or be shown your true pathway though this lifetime.

I've prepared several visualizations for you. These are some of my favourites and the ways I've found that work best for the beginner. If you want to, you can record these meditations onto a CD. If you feel able to, embellish the journey with any additional details that come to you. You can of course buy ready-made meditation CDs for this, but the sound of your own voice, whilst a little strange at first, will generate a closer link with the words than a stranger's will.

Once you have your CD, you might find that on the first several attempts all that seems to happen is that you fall asleep. If that's the case, don't worry. All it means is that you're learning to relax, which is a very important step in its own right. And even while you're asleep the meditation will still work and you'll wake up feeling very good. You might not remember anything you were shown, but the information will still work on your subconscious, boosting that ever-important store of positive energy.

Try out whichever of the following visualizations appeals to you or use them all. The choice is yours.

The way to try these visualizations is to pause where I've paused, close your eyes and 'see' that part very clearly before opening your eyes again and reading the next part. Each time you open your eyes you must refresh the whole meditation, starting from the beginning, before carrying on with the next part. This might seem like a slightly difficult test of memory, but it's actually a device to send you deeper into meditation. The more you have to concentrate on the visualization, the easier it will be for you to reach the dimension you're aiming for. By repeating the whole thing each time you'll be setting the story into your mind, until in the end it becomes seamless and continuous and easier and easier to 'be there'.

It's very important to really 'see' everything in your mind as vividly as you possibly can. 'See' every leaf and petal and grass stalk, and 'smell' everything too. 'Touch' as many things as you can, and really 'feel' the textures.

If you find it difficult to concentrate, then just keep going back to the start and eventually you'll get there.

These visiualizations may seem a little fanciful in places, but have been tried and tested and carefully designed to be the easiest way of switching off your mundane worries and also of reaching your inner child, who has always known full well how to speak with angels.

At some point in each meditation you may find that your subconscious takes over and you are suddenly deep into the 'other realm'. If so, just go with it. Or you may find that your imagination provides the rest of the visualization and it differs from the written words, in which case again just accept that your subconscious knows best and go with it.

Once you achieve deep relaxation and are able to retreat from the real world, you will be able to access and be accessible to angels. By the time you've met your

Guardian Angel, on the beach or in the woods, etc., you can stay and talk to them or you can come back to reality, depending on how you feel. You may find yourself waking up. If so, that's fine. Trust that you'll be able to sustain it longer next time. If you find yourself being taken off by the angel to talk and learn, that's fine too. Because you have made contact with your Guardian, you'll be quite safe and be brought back when it's right for you.

THE BEACH AND THE DRAGON

Imagine you're walking barefoot along a beach. The sun is warm on your back.

The sea is turquoise and clear, with little ripples of pure white foam on the caps. The gentle waves come towards you and then retreat. They make a gushing noise as they ebb and flow.

You look down at your footprints and see that there are multi-coloured pebbles and shells dotted in the sand.

You're near the water's edge. The stones and shells are painted wet and shiny and bright by the lazy seawater. As the water slides away the sun immediately tries to dry them.

You can smell the ozone of the sea, sharp and refreshing, and hear the more distant waves as they break.

You can hear the sound of the tide dragging its way through the pebbles as a soft shushing noise.

High overhead the sky is a brilliant blue and gulls soar around, flashing white wings. You can hear their cries.

All the sounds you hear fill you with peace.

You continue to walk. You look down and can see your bare feet making prints in the wet sand as you walk onwards.

As you walk, look around. See the ocean, which looks infinite. In the distance you can see its surface sparkling here and there like diamonds.

A small white sailboat bobs along out there, but you cannot hear any people.

You see a hump on the sand ahead. As you get closer you can hear breathing. You see metallic scales gleaming in the sun and see plumes of smoke rising. You realize this is a sleeping dragon.

You are not afraid, because in this realm nothing can harm you. The dragon sleeps on and you're able to walk around him.

You see his sharp claws flexing as they clench grains of sand and pebbles in time with his breathing. You see how his shiny scales neatly overlap each other. You see his nostrils opening and closing as he breathes, a small puff of smoke coming from each one. He smells hot.

Now the dragon opens his eyes, which shine red as rubies. You feel no fear. He sits up and breathes on you. His warm breath blows away any lingering doubt or darkness from you and you feel lighter and happier.

The dragon goes back to sleep. You walk on, leaving him behind.

Far ahead you can see a figure coming towards you. As yet you can't make out any details except how beautiful and white it is.

As the figure comes closer still you feel intrigued and welcomed.

You can see the figure more clearly now. It is a man and he's wearing long, brilliant white robes. He has beautiful white wings folded against his back and making a curved shape above his head.

Now you can see his face, as he is only feet away. He has a gentle yet powerful face. It's almost feminine, but also strong. He is holding out a hand to you.

As he takes your hand, you are able to speak. You ask his name and he tells you immediately.

The two of your walk hand in hand along the sand. Your angel takes flight and you soar with him up into the blue sky.

There is no fear. You are completely safe. His hand holds yours firmly. You look around and can see gulls flying level with you.

You look down and you can see the beach below and the water glittering in the sunlight. You pass over trees and you can look down at their tops from above. Your angel starts to talk to you.

THE COUNTRY LANE AND THE CRYSTAL STAIRCASE

You're walking alone along a quiet country lane. It's warm and sunny. It's very peaceful, with no traffic at all, and in the centre of the lane the grass has grown through.

You look down. The surface of the lane is of packed earth rather than tarmac, but you can see that on your feet you have stout walking boots that shrug off the dust and occasional patches of mud.

It was raining a while ago and there are still puddles of water here and there. These puddles glint in the sunshine.

There are some tall trees at the side of the lane and their leaves drip with water from the rain. The drips fall into the puddles with soft plinking sounds, causing ripples that ebb and flow as you watch them.

There is a hedgerow too, dotted with wild roses that are pale pink and delicate. Purple flowers nestle in the grass verge.

You can smell cut grass from the hay fields beyond the hedgerow and the tangy, slightly metallic smell of the recent rain.

You can hear a soft buzzing in the flowers and when you look you can see bumble bees wobbling around among the flowers' faces, settling here and there to drink the sweet nectar.

You continue to walk, watching your feet as they leave slight imprints in the earth of the road. You look around, seeing the hedges and flowers. Purple butterflies accompany you, fluttering around above your head.

You come to a gate and push it open. You walk through into a field. The grass is long and wet and it wraps around your legs, but it doesn't feel cold, just refreshing.

A violet mist is forming in the centre of the field where it dips down into a hollow. You walk through the mist and feel all negative emotions and doubts being washed away.

You come to a pool. The water is green and translucent and you can see silver fish in its depths.

There's a waterfall gushing into it over granite rocks. You can hear its rushing, tumbling sound and it draws you to it.

Next to the waterfall is a stairway made entirely of clear crystal. You look upwards. It seems to go on and on. You can't see the top as it curves away.

You walk up the crystal stairway, up and up.

In the distance you can see the summit now and at the top you see a figure starting to come slowly down the stairway to meet you. It is just a golden shape, glowing with light. You feel happy to see it, knowing it brings you good news.

You walk a little faster, keen to reach the figure. As you get closer you see he has long curly dark hair and a wonderful smile. His eyes are green.

He shines golden in the sun, and with inner light. He holds out his arms and you walk into them. You ask him his name out loud and he answers immediately.

You walk together down the crystal stairway. In the distance below you can see the pool sparkling like a small silver coin. You realize you can see for miles, but you are not afraid.

Your angel starts to talk to you.

THE WOODLAND AND THE FAIRY CASTLE

You are in the depths of woodland. It's a soft spring day, warm but not hot. You look down at your feet and see that you are wearing leather shoes.

Ahead stretches a narrow, curving pathway lined with scintillating bluebells, their heads nodding. The surface of the path has gnarly tree roots sticking out here and there and you have to watch your footing.

You set off down the path which calls to you with welcome. Overhead the sky is blue, punctuated with pure white fluffy clouds.

The trees either side of the path have fresh new leaves just opening. The leaves are acid green and create shadows on the path. As you look up at them you see something flitting across the branches. It could be a squirrel or a bird, it doesn't matter to you.

As you walk you start to get warm, but there's a breeze blowing through the trees that keeps you cool. You look down and see knots of yellow primroses among the blue of the bluebells.

You can hear the breeze as it makes a soughing noise in the treetops. You can hear birdsong in the trees.

You can smell the woody scent of the trees and the musky scent of the topsoil below your feet, which is composed of leaves from hundreds of years.

As you turn a corner, there in front of you in a clearing is a gorgeous fairy castle. It is tiny, as befits its occupants, but still impressive. Tiny minarets are studded with creamy pearls and the gateway is encrusted with diamonds. The walls themselves are covered in arching rainbows.

As you get nearer the rainbows fall over you like sweet-smelling rain, flushing any fears and cares away with multiple colours. You kneel down and let the wonderful rainbow colours envelop you.

Feeling renewed and confident, you walk on along the bluebell path.

As the path unwinds ahead of you, you catch glimpses of someone approaching. You are not afraid; in fact you're excited about meeting this person.

Tantalizing glimpses are seen as the figure wends its way through the bluebells towards you.

You round the final bend and there he is – a being, all clad in blue to blend with the bluebells, reaching out to you. You feel love surging over you.

He has blond hair and vivid blue eyes that reflect the bluebells again. You take his hands and unstoppable love flows through you like water. You ask his name and he tells you.

You stand and stare into his eyes and he speaks without talking. You share telepathy with this being.

THE QUIET PLACE WITHIN AND THE UNICORN

After you've relaxed your body, you can't feel it at all. It's just as it if it has melted away. You realize that you are comprised of just energy, no substance.

Now your core being is sinking through the layers, going deep inside your energetic body. You sink lower and lower until you reach the centre.

Here you find yourself entering a room. The room is completely lined with silk fabrics of many colours. The walls are draped with them.

On the floor of the room there are cushions of all shapes and sizes. They are gold, red, purple and pink and each one is ornate with embroidery and small precious stones.

Your energy floats to the floor and rests on the cushions.

There is no sound at first and then you start to hear a rhythmic drumming. It's very quiet at first and then, as it gets louder, you understand that it is your own heartbeat.

The air around you is filled with scents and perfumes. You sense more than hear soft footfalls behind you. You turn around, and there, walking through the cushions towards you, is a pure white unicorn. His spiral horn glistens with magic.

The unicorn settles down beside you, tucking his dainty feet under his legs. He rests his head on you and as he does your energy starts to pulsate to the beat of your heart.

You feel your energy body changing, shimmering with colour after colour. Each colour change lifts your energy higher and higher, until you feel like bursting with power and happiness.

The unicorn slowly vanishes and you start to feel a vibration in the air around you. Warmth spreads over you and you can feel your energetic body starting to glow.

You feel enveloped in golden energy, much more powerful than your own, and the unconditional love it brings you makes your energy tingle.

An angelic being is all around you. It is you and you are it. You ask the being its name and it tells you immediately.

The energy starts to show you visions.

More Advanced Methods of Meditation

You may decide to study a more advanced method of meditation so I've listed here some of the better-known types. What soon becomes clear is that meditation is part of all religious practice under one title or another and in one form or another.

Taoist

The Taoist way of meditating doesn't actually differ a great deal from other methods except that one should first develop a 'Taoist way of being'. A Taoist practises oneness with all things of nature, learning to accept what is and merge with the world and all its parts and happenings rather than striving to use or control nature or change those events not seen as desirable.

Christian

A Christian will use the texts of the Bible as a way of focusing the mind in an effort to discover the true meaning and being of their creator. Merely reading the Bible can produce a meditative state of mind. Other forms of meditation are achieved by the use of repetitive prayer, for example the saying of the rosary.

Islamic

There are many branches of Islam, but to take an example, Shia and Sunni Muslims use Salat as the basis for meditation. This is the reciting five times daily of devotional prayers. On special occasions they also use Wajib Salat, a form which is reserved for special occasions. Sunnah Salat and Nafi Salat are two further optional forms of devotional prayer that can be recited at specific times.

Jain

The religion of Jainism believes that meditation of the highest kind can be practised through self-denial. For instance, Jains often meditate outside, naked, whatever the weather, and sometimes standing up.

Hindu/Yoga

Hindu meditation is basically the same as many other forms of spiritual meditation, but was one of the first to be developed. In yoga, posture is very important, as is the control of breathing. Energy, or *prana*, is channelled by chanting mantras, such as the classic 'Om'.

Wiccan

To use this method of meditation you'll need a picture of a pentagram, or five-pointed star, with a single point at the top, two at the bottom and one on each side. This symbol has no original links to the occult, as some may think. The aim is to use it to focus on as you begin to meditate, concentrating on one point at a time. This method is similar to the system used by some hypnotherapists, where the patient is asked to stare at an image.

Chakra Meditation

This form of meditation is specifically designed to clear the chakras of the body. To facilitate it you should sit down, clear your mind and concentrate on each of the seven chakras in turn. It's helpful to picture each one as a tightly budded flower that is gradually unfurled. Each chakra should be closed down again to its bud form after the meditation is complete.

Mirror and Candlelight Meditation

Another way to bring angels closer is to use the mirror and candlelight method. Stand in front of a mirror in a room lit only by candlelight. Stare into the mirror and control your breathing, making it very even and regular. If you are successful, then after a time an angel's image will appear in the mirror, superimposed over your own reflection. At this point you can ask it questions.

Finishing a Meditation

When you exit a meditation, take your time and don't rush to get back into the world too soon. Just breathe deeply for a few minutes and enjoy your relaxed body.

While you're doing this, close yourself down by picturing your energy as a fan and imagining the segments all folding and closing together to form a tight impenetrable block.

All you need to do after that is to have a nice long drink of water, as meditation can cause a little dehydration. Imagine the water to be liquid crystal and it will leave you refreshed and revitalized.

MESSAGES THROUGH MEDITATION

During all of these meditations, keep a very open mind when it comes to hearing angels speak. At first you'll probably hear just a few disjointed words and you may not grasp their full meaning, or you might see flashes of an image but not be able to identify it. Another problem might be that as soon as you get one of these momentary messages or visions you'll rip yourself out of the meditation, because at first your mind is straining so hard for them that it will ping you back to reality like a snapping piece of elastic as soon as it hears or sees something. But have patience and write down everything you see or hear on a special notepad, because over time your technique will improve and the scraps of messages and visions will start to form something that makes sense. These little messages and signs are all meant to point you in the right direction and in time you'll start to recognize the areas of your life that they pertain to and will have the trust to act on all of them.

Once your brain has understood that it needs to maintain the meditative state despite being startled by words and pictures, you'll be able to enter into a two-way conversation, asking questions of your angel and getting answers immediately.

Remember this isn't just for today, it's for the rest of your life, and in five years' time you'll look back in awe at how much you and your life have changed since you began living through angels.

All of this concentration and excitement can leave you a little drained, but there are therapies available to help you recuperate and relax, thereby enhancing your functionality in the world you have to live in. The therapies in the next chapter can be used to further your spiritual progress or simply recharge your emotional batteries.

CHAPTER 6
ANGEL THERAPIES

There are many different forms of angel-based therapies and they can all be useful additions to your journey to attune more closely to the realms of angels. It never does any harm to take every opportunity to transform some of your more negative energy or top up the positive energy you've already gained. Talking about angels, thinking about angels and undergoing angel-based therapies with like-minded positive therapists and readers are all good ways to expand your possibilities. There are so many available, however, that it can be a confusing choice to make, so I've listed some of them here with a testimonial for each one as well as my own opinion to give you an idea of what to expect and what you might gain from them.

ANGEL THERAPY®

Angel Therapy is a non-denominational spiritual healing method inspired by angels in communication with Doreen Virtue. Qualified therapists can be found all over the world and there's a list of where to find them on Doreen's website (*see Resources*). The healing involves working with a person's Guardian Angel and the archangels to heal and harmonize every aspect of their life. It helps clients to more clearly receive divine guidance from the creator and from angels, bringing them back on their spiritual path in a way that is non-threatening and non-judgemental.

To me this therapy is a safe bet, as it seems to work for pretty much everyone. Doreen Virtue is very well known for her ability to communicate directly with angels and although you may not be lucky enough to be able to have a session with her personally, anyone trained correctly in her methods should be able to help you.

Mary, of London, told me:

I was in danger of going right off the rails when I was 16 and I turned to this therapy out of sheer desperation. I had no family, no money, and was about to become homeless. I was so desperate that I was thinking of turning to prostitution as a way of getting by in the world. After my session I realized there were a lot more options than I'd seen before. I think angels opened my eyes. I found there were grants I could apply for that I hadn't known about and training I could do that wouldn't cost me anything. Most of all, I came to value myself too much to sell my body for money. I'm now studying at college and hope to start working in the computer industry.

ANGEL ENERGY HEALING FOR THE DYING

In this kind of therapy the practitioner actually opens their body to an angel, or sometimes a host of angels, to bring messages of comfort and healing to a person who has been told by the medical profession that they only have a very short time to live.

To me this seems a very specialized therapy and is the only one of its kind that I found. Sometimes it brings a miraculous cure, but it seems to be mainly focused on bringing peace and acceptance and comfort to someone who is about to leave this world.

Bill, from Taunton in the UK, told me:

I'd been given just a few months to live because I was suffering from pancreatic cancer. As you can imagine, I was terrified. The fear was overwhelming me and stopping me from making the most of the time I had left. All I could see was a ticking clock, counting down my life. I was also worried about my family and yet I couldn't concentrate on tying up the loose ends to protect them.

The treatment was amazing. I could feel the presence of angels in the room and peace came over me. My fear of dying receded and I was told I could choose the time of my passing, which was a great comfort.

I know now that when the time comes I'll be able to have all my family round me and we'll all be prepared. I don't want to die, of course, but I can cope with the prospect now instead of being paralyzed with anticipation.

ANGEL THERAPY WITH A MEDIUM

Angel therapy with a medium is a gentle afterlife-affirming way to connect to loved ones who have passed over, through angels. It's designed especially for those who weren't able to say goodbye to the dying. Angels are unconditionally loving entities and are here to help in every area of life, including those times when we're enduring terrible losses.

I know that when we lose a loved one we often have many questions to ask and that at the same time we're also dealing with grief, and possibly anger at having lost the person. Angels won't always be permitted to answer our questions, but receiving some proof that their loved one still exists and is happy and safe can be enough for the grieving to be able to move on.

Sharon, of Bristol in the UK, told me about her experience:

I knew my mum was ill but I didn't expect her to go so suddenly, while I wasn't with her. I couldn't accept that she'd leave without sending me a sign, so I prayed for one, but it wasn't until I had a reading with an angelically connected medium that I got three signs in one day. In the early hours I felt a need to watch the sky and a shooting star swept across the night right in front of me. Then, as I was thinking about Mum later during the day, a whole load of items suddenly fell off the supermarket shelves, even though there was no one near them. Then I found a note that my mum had sent me months previously lying on my bed. I know I threw that note in the trash, so there was no way it could have arrived there by itself.

ANGEL CHANNELLING

In this kind of therapy, the reader channels information direct from your angels and says the exact words your angel wants you to hear, as if they themselves were speaking to you. This can be in the form of answers to direct questions or it can be general information that your angels want you to have, usually referring to your path in life.

Channelled messages from your angels offer gentle and loving guidance and support for all aspects of your life, from day-to-day advice to assistance with decision making and life direction. But whatever they concern, they are always loving and supportive, If your life isn't quite on track, angels won't tell you off, give you bad news or something to worry about. Rather, they will gently and positively guide you to make the best of the opportunities you have to get back on track. And they will lovingly persist with a message until it is received and acted upon.

I would say that this therapy is good if a person needs to hear information in a way that convinces them it comes directly from angels. The unusual turns of phrase used in these readings can often provide something convincing that a person can grasp and hold onto.

Jessie, of Seattle in the USA, said:

I was astonished by the speech that came tumbling out of the reader's mouth. I was expecting maybe a few words, but what I got was far more. I'd been searching for a direction in life, but also for some confirmation that I wasn't alone. The angel said things that the reader couldn't have known about, and it didn't even sound like her voice. It was in what I'd describe as old-fashioned language, and the message meant the world to me. I came away feeling supported and loved and I think my whole life will change.

ANGEL CRYSTAL READINGS

In these readings, the reader first dowses with a pendulum to discover which crystal your angel vibrates to and then uses a sample of that crystal to bring your Guardian Angel in. Once the angel is there, you can ask questions of it. After the session you can take the crystal home so that you can use it to communicate with your angel yourself. The reader will also provide you with a name for your angel so that you can use it to call your angel to you.

I have a special affinity with crystals, so I like this therapy very much and it's one I have used myself many times. Even at home on my own, when I have a new crystal that 'chose me', I find just holding it in my hand can help me attain a deeper state of meditation than without it. This therapy is also useful if you're not confident about contacting angels on your own yet, because you're able to maintain a slight connection to the therapist through the crystal, which has shared both your energies.

Alison, of Bamburg in Germany, told me:

The reading itself was amazing, but what amazed me most was that I'd been trying to connect with my angel for years without success, because I found it impossible to meditate, and after the session I was able to do it instantly. When I got home I was able to meditate for two hours solid.

I discovered that my angel was called Shamir, which means 'hope'. I will never be without hope now.

ANGEL TOUCH REIKI

Reiki is a natural healing system where the practitioner gently lays their hands on the client or holds their hands just above them. It uses energy to adjust the client's own body's energy patterns in order to help them reach a level where their own bodies can heal themselves and return to normal function or a better balance. During a treatment the client remains fully dressed and either lies on a therapy bed or sits in a chair.

Reiki is not about faith. It is about using universal energy to support us or our animals. Just as our bodies need food and water to provide energy for us to function, so we need universal energy in our system in order to thrive. With Reiki you may experience a range of sensations: warmth, coolness, tingling, pulsing or maybe a sense of weightlessness and peace.

I like these gentle therapies, as they make you feel cosseted somehow, as if you have indeed been touched by an angel. Angel Touch Reiki would be especially good for someone who felt taken for granted and unimportant in their everyday lives.

Bridget, from Dublin in Ireland, had this to say about it:

I'd been having a very stressful time at work, and there had been some sexual harassment in the office. Consequently I'd had to take long-term sick leave and I really was unsure whether I could return or not. Another side effect had been panic attacks.

Joanne offered me Angelic Reiki, and she told me that the energy in the room during the treatment was significantly different from usual and felt more powerful than at many other times. She called in the angels, and as she finished her welcoming she said she became aware that angels were standing around me, one at each shoulder and one by each foot. She said they raised their arms, their fingers almost touching, and she could see I had risen up out of my body at that point and was almost completely wrapped in a gold shimmering aura-type blanket which fell over my head, face, arms and feet.

Next, blue shimmers arrived, joining the angels and towering over them. (Joanne says that Sirians have energy akin to that of angels and that we are most aware of them as dolphin energy, so it may be that these were Sirian beings.) They were finally joined by fairies, which Joanne said danced around me.

> *I wasn't closed to such things and after the healing I told*
> *her, 'That's odd, because as the Reiki healing progressed, an-*
> *gels and then fairies came to mind.' I'm not saying that I*
> *saw them, but I guess somehow I knew they were there.*

HYPNOSIS

Hypnosis is a state of deep relaxation, just like meditation, but in which you are guided and encouraged by a
hypnotist. You won't be asleep and you'll be able to hear
everything the hypnotherapist says to you. You'll be aware
of where you really are but it won't impact on you. You'll
be able to come out of the session at any time if you want
to, but you usually won't feel that you do want to.

Being under hypnosis is very much like having a powerful daydream. It's how you feel first thing in the morning
in those few delicious minutes before you're fully awake
or in those relaxing moments just before you fall asleep,
when you're deliciously drowsy and carefree. Being hyp-
notized is actually a natural state of being. It's a state that
happens when we're switched off and not really thinking
about anything at all. When undertaken by a qualified
and skilled therapist, it can give us access to our subconscious mind.

Angel Hypnosis

With angel hypnosis, you'll have a hypnosis session in
which you'll be given a guided relaxation and an aura
and chakra clearing in order to release you from your

negative thoughts or emotional challenges. This removes low vibrational frequencies so you can call in the highest vibrational guidance. If you are too loaded mentally, emotionally or physically with problems, you may require more extensive work before you are able to establish a permanent relationship with your spiritual guardians. A good hypnotherapist can uncover the reasons why someone is overwhelmed by negative energy and help them change it around to positivity.

Once you are ready and at peace within yourself, you will be taken through a guided meditation that changes your brainwave patterns to a deep level of consciousness, with alpha and delta combined, where you will be able to contact your guides or Guardian Angel. You will become aware of the messages that they are offering you and these will be right for you at that time. The mind communicates through symbols and you will be helped to understand the symbolism that you are being offered.

After every session you will be able to go home with the most profound message for you and you may also be offered some special healing from the angelic realms.

This connection with your Guardian Angel or guide will change your level of consciousness and will open the communication link between you and your highest level of guidance for the rest of your life, ensuring that you can be in tune with your soul. It is like reclaiming a talent we used to have but have lost in the materialistic present.

I've always been a naturally good subject for hypnosis and have found it of value. It's always good to learn more about yourself, and if you sometimes feel as though you don't know who you are or why you're here at all, this would be a good therapy for you too.

It's only fair to say that after my initial experience of hypnotic regression I did get a bit stuck in the past life that was revealed. The grief that I felt when I recalled the situation I'd gone through was far greater than the hypno-therapist was expecting and I couldn't shake it off. After four years of suffering from it, I found a therapist who called in angels before a session. She was also very much more experienced in past-life regression and its effects than my initial hypnotherapist. By bringing in my angels during the session she was able to take me through a cord-cutting procedure whereby I was able to let go of the pain without letting go of the love or the memories. Whilst I think that in my case the first session was meant to 'go wrong' so that I could fulfil my role in life, it was also necessary after a while to cut the cords of the pain of that life so that I could function more fully in this lifetime.

Hypnosis and Meditation

As well as learning more about your past and present, under the auspices of a good hypnotherapist you'll get to know the feel of the state you're trying to achieve during meditation, so if you haven't succeeded in reaching it yet, you'll know what you're looking for.

I liken it to when I was learning equestrian dressage. I was a novice and so was my horse. There's a movement known as a half-pass where the horse steps sideways as opposed to forwards or backwards and I couldn't get it right. My horse didn't seem to understand what I was asking for and I couldn't seem to discover exactly how to explain it to him using the conventional aids. Then I had a ride on a horse that was already trained to half-pass. All I had to do, under instruction, was to 'press the right buttons' and he automatically performed the movement perfectly. Then, when I got back on my own horse, I knew what the movement felt like and so I was able to communicate to him what I wanted much more effectively than before.

ANGEL READINGS

These are readings using one of the many packs of angel cards available, but performed by a professional psychic rather than yourself. Such a reading will often involve the answers to choices that you've been called to make or will be called to make further down the line. It should end up with you feeling that you are never alone, can always call for help and are loved. An angel reading should never be anything but positive and if it does throw up any future problems, it should give you the ways you need to circumvent or deal with them when they arise.

You can always tell a good angel card reader because they give you the feeling that you're ready for anything. If you leave a session feeling depressed, then you can be sure the reader wasn't genuine.

I talked to Kate, of Hull in the UK, about her reading. She said:

> *I was a bit concerned about what I might be told. I certainly didn't want to hear about anything bad coming up – my imagination could supply that for me! But it wasn't like that at all. It was gentle and reassuring and I came out feeling lighter and supported at the same time.*

SOUL ANGEL THERAPY

This is a form of angelic reading that concentrates on putting you in touch with the angels who have dealt with you in past lives. Sometimes, if you're blocked in trying to raise your vibration, it can be due to a past-life trauma. Realizing and releasing these traumas can accomplish a very swift turnaround in this lifetime.

I believe that anyone who doesn't know anything about their soul history is as limited as someone who suffers from amnesia in this lifetime. I call it 'amnesia of the soul'. If you have any interest in discovering who you really are by discovering who you really were, this is the angel therapy for you.

Gemma, from Cannock in the UK, told me her experience:

I was so excited to get the information regarding my past life as a nun, as it resonated with a lot of things that had gone on in my life up to that point.

The reading made a lot of difference to my life and explained why I had so many blockages, especially with regard to relationships.

Since I have begun to understand what made me who I am today, I have felt my angel drawing ever closer. I'm sure I'll be able to make the connection now.

QUANTUM ANGEL HEALING®

With this treatment, angels and other messengers of God come forward and help to find the cause and solution for a problem or disease. They communicate with the quantum angel practitioner and at the same time let their divine energy flow through their hands to the client. During treatments, clients can feel warmth and tingling or see colours, angels and light. With the help of this new angelic healing formula, old energies, patterns and belief systems are transformed in a magical way. Through Quantum Angel Healing, all possible sources of pain, illness, confusion, low energy or feelings of being stuck or blocked are addressed. With this therapy, you will be able to manifest the life of your dreams.

I feel this is an especially good therapy for someone who has tried several other therapies and not found one that suits them. Dealing with issues on a quantum level means that no stone remains unturned.

Mary, of Arizona in the USA, had this to say about it:

Without being really aware of it, I'd been an empath all my life. When I was in school, I could always feel the fears and pains of other students and wished I could be their friend and help them. But because of my intuitive gifts, people around me called me a weirdo and I had a lot of hurt in my life. Since childhood, I had gained a lot of weight and had many trust issues. My relationships with men were either a nightmare or simply not happening at all. I tried to change my life and was looking for answers. I paid a lot of money to fortune tellers, psychics, and card readers, who always promised me the love of my life was coming soon. Finally, one day I found Quantum Angel Healing® on the Internet. I could feel that it was truly inspired by angels and could sense that it was something new and special. So I made an appointment with Eva-Maria Mora, the founder of this healing modality.

I'd never experienced anything like it in my whole life. Through direct communication with angels, Eva-Maria identified and revealed the origin of all my problems. She explained that my current life issues related to past lives when I was persecuted for my gifts as a healer and that I had a lot of painful memories from this energy still stored in my system. I understood that this energy needed to be transformed and my old pain needed to be healed before I could really live the life that I desired. The angels explained that I had established belief systems and DNA programming that caused me to experience painful life situations over and over again.

I asked the angels many questions and received a lot of insight about myself and my life. The most important part of my session was the actual hands-on energy treatment, when the angelic healing energy flowed through Eva-Maria's hands. My body started to tingle and everything felt warm. Then it felt as though the angels pulled something out of my solar plexus chakra and also worked on my head and my heart. I saw a lot of colors and pictures during the process and even had some tears rolling down my cheek. I've never felt so light and happy in my life. I knew immediately that the treatment was successful. Afterwards I felt different.

That was six months ago and since then I've lost 40 pounds and had some profound changes in my life. I feel truly blessed. People are treating me in a totally different way. I now feel ready for a relationship and I have trust in my own abilities. Thank you, angels!

ANGEL COACHING

This is said to be a powerful conversation and support system that empowers you to find unexpected reserves of energy and shake off tension and stress. Through it, angels can help you nurture your creativity and spirituality and clarify your life choices and direction. Angel coaching can answer your questions and enlighten you about why you're here and where you are going.

I believe this is a good therapy for people who are facing difficult choices or feel they are standing at an important crossroads in their lives and lacking the confidence to choose a direction.

Jane, from Cambridge in the UK, told me this about her session:

Prior to learning about angels and spirits from Kylie, I'd felt that something was missing from my life and I'd had a lot of unanswered questions like 'Why does everything bad happen to me?' and 'What have I done wrong?' This may sound silly to some people; however, after meeting my Guardian Angel on the course run by Kylie I started to think and feel differently, and then Kylie kindly read my soul. This was a smart investment and for a few weeks I felt an inner peace which gave me the free time and concentration I needed to get my life back on track.

With the help of Kylie and her ability to comfort, provide inner peace and subconsciously build my confidence, I now feel that I'm a very lucky person who has lots to look forward to every day and who has the support of the angels and spirits who are there with me. I would like to give Kylie a big thank-you for helping me to get my life back on track and for teaching me to understand how angels and spirits can be my friends.

ANGEL COLOUR THERAPY

Here the therapist will look at your aura and channel the colours that are right for you to wear and have around you to make and keep a connection to your angel. The colours that are found will be used to complement your angel's energy. Sometimes an existing aura photo can be used.

I feel that colour is a vastly underrated factor in our lives, and there's no doubt that following angelic advice on what colours to wear and when to wear them can be invaluable.

Paris, from Kaupang in Norway, had a lovely experience through this therapy:

> *I'd been trying to get a new job for months, but I always lost my nerve at the interviews. During the therapy my angel told me to wear some turquoise at the next one. I was told that it would inspire confidence in my prospective employer. I really believed it, which made a difference anyway, but for whatever reason the interview went really well and I was offered the job there and then.*

ANGEL ART

In this kind of angel communication the artist creates a painting of your Guardian Angel. I have had a portrait done by Patrick Gamble, who is internationally recognized as the top artist in this field. When he works, Patrick often sees many divine beings around a person, but he paints the one that comes to the fore, and this is their unique guardian.

Diane, of Cornwall in the UK, wrote to tell me:

I first heard about Patrick and how wonderful he was from someone I met three years ago and I kept thinking I must make contact with him, but life kept preventing it. I'm a great believer in timing, and when I moved to Cornwall two years ago, I remembered he came from that area and in my piles of paperwork I discovered his leaflet. He was busy moving at that time and still we did not manage to connect, but somehow I trusted the situation and thought, 'When the time is right it will happen,' and left it at that.

I was living in an 1860s cottage on the east side of Bodmin Moor. It was built into the hill, with wonderful views over the village below and just the sound of the river and the birds. As a holistic therapist, I'd imagined I'd be able to offer patients a perfect retreat there. Little did I realize that I had bought a place full of trapped spirits who were creating lots of disturbances, mainly in the form of water coming through ceilings and very unsettling emotional feelings for me and the various friends who came to stay. They were having emotional outbursts and lots of things were going wrong, so I finally sought the help of Patrick. He, by this time, quite by 'chance', had moved very near to the village where I lived. He told me that before he knew where I was he'd passed the end of my single-track lane and thought he didn't like the nature of the energy in that area! So, when I invited him to come to my place, he knew immediately there were energy problems.

On the day he arrived, as soon as he emerged from his van, I had such a sense of relief. He gave me a feeling of security immediately. He was so down to earth, yet obvi-

ously highly spiritual – a brilliant combination. He chatted away over coffee about varying things, sharing his experiences with me. But all the time I sensed he was bringing healing to the place. Then he got to work with his paints. When he had finished I was amazed to see a strong-looking spirit guide staring me right in the eye – a very powerful presence, created in oils. The picture of this spirit guide, who had been brought through by Patrick's connection to angels, was to be left in my cottage to give protection. I kept looking at the image and feeling such courage and strength – it was a perfect stabilizer and I had the feeling that its presence would ward off anything negative.

I'd had my property on the market for a number of months at that point and hadn't had much response. That very afternoon the estate agent phoned to say some people wanted to view the property three weeks from that day. They duly came down to Cornwall and made an offer.

MIRROR ANGEL READINGS

The ability to do these readings is something I was given by the Master Path Angel in order to help me in my seed-planting role. What I do is tune into your Guardian Angel and create a digital portrait of it. The colours and attitude of the angel give me answers to your problems. I call these 'Mirror Angels' because they tend to appear as a reflection of what your true soul looks like to those who can *see*. I do these readings for *Take 5* magazine in Australia and *Soul & Spirit* magazine in the UK, as well as privately.

Suz, from Wickford in the UK, sent me this comment when she received her angel portrait and reading:

> *I am absolutely gobsmacked and exhilarated by this beautiful angel. I am sitting here totally overawed and with my mouth open! Part of me wants to cry, but the angel has truly taken my breath away.*

AUTOMATIC WRITING

Automatic writing is when you produce written words that you didn't form consciously. It's a form of channelling where you bring through information and answers from the spirit world, or in this case, from your angels. You become their tool and you have no knowledge of what you've written until you look at it afterwards.

This form of connecting with angels can be very successful with people who are too sceptical to allow their energy to connect directly with them. It can also work with people who are too regimented to let go of the control of their mind. Automatic writing can seem safer to them because although a part of their brain is turned over to the possibility of communication, they can still function in the real world while they are doing it.

How Do You Do It?

You can use pencil or pen and paper or even your computer keyboard to actually produce the writing. Would you like to try it now?

Sit with a pen or pencil held loosely in your hand over a sheet of paper or sit relaxed with your fingers poised over the keyboard and close your eyes. You'll need to place yourself in a receptive frame of mind by doing the counting and breathing meditation outlined earlier (*see pages 96–97*).

When you feel ready, either ask a specific question of your angels or say that you'll be happy to receive any guidance they feel is appropriate.

Don't open your eyes, just let your hand start working. It may take a while, so just wait calmly.

When you do start, write as fast as you can so that the flow is as continuous as possible.

Keep asking questions until the writing stops.

When you're sure you've finished, look at what has been written and see if you can discern a message there. There are physics out there who will do this for you if your own success is limited.

My own best example of automatic writing was when I was penning my book about my past-life experience. I had come to a part that was tricky because I wanted to know about what had happened to someone after I had died in that life. I recall, and so does Tony, that I was actually sitting watching *Coronation Street* on the TV (it seems that soaps can send you into a state of meditation!), when my right hand started writing without my putting any conscious thought into it. To my amazement, when

Tony and I looked at what was written on the paper, it all made perfect sense. This is certainly something I would try again if I needed help to connect to my angels.

GROUP MEDITATION

This is when a group of like-minded people get together and sit in a circle to go into meditation together, rather than one person trying to do it alone. There is usually a leader who guides the others into a meditative state.

Just as with the power of prayer, many people together can create more powerful energy than one person alone. Even if you've never been able to meditate deliberately before, you may well get swept along in a group dynamic.

How Do You Do It?

Group meditation is very common nowadays and the local press or your nearest New Age store will probably be a good place to look if you're interested in joining a group. There may well be several available, and if so, the best way is to give a few of them a try and see how you get on.

Amazing things can happen during group meditation. I've known spontaneous past-life regression to occur, with two people sharing memories of a life they once lived together. These two were obviously meant to meet up, due to their past-life connection, and of course it was no accident that they were drawn to the same circle on the same day. Angels work in mysterious ways!

Little preparation is necessary for group meditation, as this is all taken care of at the time. However, you should be prepared to share your experiences of the meditation with the other members of the circle. Don't worry about this – as always, talking about angels and spiritual matters with like-minded people encourages the right kind of energy, just as discussing negative issues encourages the wrong kind.

By this point you should be in touch with your angels, and one of the first things to try and find out is their name, which they're usually willing to give. It's much easier to develop a relationship if you have a name to use, just as it would be with a person. From there you can go on to communicate with them more easily...

CHAPTER 7

COMMUNICATING WITH ANGELS

By now you should feel that you have a connection with angels, both your own Guardian Angel and Master Path Angels, and that you're ready to ask for what you feel you need.

By now you will be fully aware every day in every aspect of your life that you must not fall into the negativity trap. You always ask your angels before you leave the house to protect you from the negative energy that's always around in the modern world. You avoid talking to negative people except when there really is no choice, especially at work. You talk to positive people as much as possible and you encourage your mind to produce endorphins by noticing the beauty that is all around you. You've become quite skilled in using angel cards, learned to meditate and given yourself a nice positive aura from using focus pictures every morning on waking and from trying lots of different angel therapies. You've perhaps tried hypnosis and automatic writing and now you feel that the time has come to get some more substantial benefits from the connection that is growing ever stronger.

This is where some major pitfalls and difficulties can start, believe it or not. Many people get this far, feel their angels around them, are sure there's two-way communication going on and ask for what they want – and then they don't get it and they just can't understand why not. So, what goes wrong?

HOW TO ASK

Asking in the right way is very important. There are six ways to do this and I would ask you to use them all:

1. During meditation, run a video in your mind of how you want your world to be. See it so clearly that it's more realistic than reality. You are creating your own reality, so make sure you get it right.

2. Write down everything you want to come to pass on an 'angelic shopping list' – a piece of paper that you keep under your pillow or beside the bed. As things on the list happen (as they will), cross them off and thank your angels for their help.

3. Take the crystals that you've learned correspond to your angels' energy and hold them in your hand while you ask for the events that you want to see happen.

4. Use your angel sanctuary to sit and quietly tell your angels what you'd like them to do. (*See Chapter 11 for how to create an angel sanctuary.*)

5. When using your focus picture, as you should continue to do, wait until you've finished saying your mantra and then close your eyes and 'see' the things you've asked for as if they are passing you by on a cosmic conveyor belt.

6. If you're going into a dangerous or uncertain situation, meditate before you go, just briefly, with the breathing and counting method, and ask for protection or assistance in being successful.

You should also always finish your requests by stating your intention that events should happen 'for the highest possible good'.

Which Angel?

Is there a specific angel for specific requests? Some people say so, but personally I've found that sometimes you'll get help from one Master Path Angel and sometimes from another and it doesn't matter which of them you ask for help. Just ask your Guardian to ask any of the Master Path Angels for help on your behalf and you can be sure your request will go to the right place.

Also, I don't believe that we can possibly know all the angels that there are by name, or which precise angel is willing and able to help us at which time. However, if you're the kind of person who focuses better if you have a name to use, then these are the Master Path angels who are most readily recognized by name and area of expertise:

- *Chamuel* is the angel to help you with relationship issues. If, for instance, you're ruining things by mistrusting and being jealous, he might help you to calm down. If you're seeking love, he might help you to be in the right place at the right time to meet the right person.

- *Gabriel* can bring calm to chaos. He is also the angel who helps with creativity, so would be good at curing writer's block or helping you devise unusual ways out of a problematic situation.

- *Jophiel* is the angel to ask for help if you're studying for exams and need some help in absorbing all that information. You could also ask him for assistance if you're preparing for a competition that means a lot to you. For instance if you want to win *The X Factor* or *American Idol*, you might ask him to make sure you don't forget the lyrics!

- *Michael* is seen as a warrior angel. He is said to be able to offer you physical protection above and beyond what your Guardian Angel can do. So, he'd be the one to ask for help if you were facing a battle or to ask for protection against accidents or crime and even in the event of having serious surgery.

- *Raphael* can help when everything seems against you. If you're ill or are in danger of losing your home, or if you feel there's nowhere to turn, he would be the one to ask for divine intervention.

- *Uriel* really doesn't like fighting and arguing, so if you're constantly having rows at home and at work, you could ask him to pour oil on your troubled waters. You could also ask him to help stop wars on a worldwide scale.

- *Zadkiel* is the social angel. If you seem to have no friends and could really do with some help to meet like-minded people who won't judge you and will be there for you, he can help.

But don't worry, because, as I said, your Guardian Angel knows whom to call on in the higher dimensions, and with your help they can do it. *You* can do it!

Whichever angel you ask, when the help arrives, and it will, don't forget to say thank you!

HOW *NOT* TO ASK

It all looks very simple, doesn't it, so how does it go wrong for people? A lot of the time it's just that they're asking for the wrong things or in the wrong way.

There are certain things you shouldn't ask for. Don't ask for money specifically and don't ask to win the lottery. Angels simply don't understand about money – why would they? It means nothing to them. If you have financial problems, just 'see' yourself feeling safe and secure without them.

Don't ask for luxury items specifically, e.g. a certain material possession. Just feel the way you would be feeling if you had that item.

If bills make you angry, that's a negative emotion which can block good events, so pay bills, when you can, with a smile and a feeling of easy release. If you begrudge the outward flow of money, you'll create a negative energy dam and will block the flow of money coming in. Energy must flow freely both in and out. Let go of money willingly and easily and it will return to you willingly and easily.

If your goal is a better job or career, never ask for someone else to suffer misfortune, e.g. get ill or lose their job, so that you can move ahead. This is negative and will stop you getting what you want as well as creating bad karma for you.

Don't get impatient. Remember how complicated things can be for your angel to arrange. Some things will take time.

Also, remember the ripple effect. Every action has an equal reaction. Remember always to finish your request with the intent that things should happen 'for the highest possible good'. This means the highest good for everyone, not just you and your loved ones.

Don't ask directly on someone else's behalf. Your Guardian Angel can't help other people. That isn't to say you can't pray for others, because what your angel *can* do is ask the other person's angel to intercede on their behalf. If possible, encourage the person who needs help to seek it directly from their own angel. It works much better that way.

Be Careful What You Wish For

You may be sure that you know what you want, but take some time to think it through and to ask for it in the most positive way. Never just ask, for instance, to be able to 'stop working'. Many events can be created to stop you working, and a lot of them will be rather nasty, such as disablements, accidents or family problems. For instance, if you ask for enough money to retire, who knows what might have to happen for you to get that money? Instead, picture yourself doing the kind of happy things you'd be doing if you didn't have to work. Perhaps picture yourself playing with your children more, relaxing with a smiling face, etc.

And whatever your request, always finish it with the intent that things should happen 'for the highest possible good'.

Know What You Really Want

Some people just don't know what they really want in order to be happy. I was like that myself. So it's very important to be able to listen to your angel as well as ask for things.

All's not lost if you really don't know what will make your life better. If you feel it's just lacking something but you don't know what, don't worry about it. Just constantly picture yourself with a smile on your face and your angel will show you the way to put that smile there. Be warned, though: your angel might have some surprises for you!

Don't Knock your Head against a Brick Wall

If the way you thought things were going to go isn't how things seem to be going, and if doors appear to be slamming in your face, then accept that you're trying to go the wrong way. Resistance never succeeds. So, be led. If you're being herded in a certain direction, just go with the flow. Your angel knows best – always!

Don't Be Rigid about How Things Will Happen

Never picture a whole series of events to lead you to your goal. If you do this you can actually end up fighting your angel, as they may need to arrange things in a different way. You might be asking for a series of events that are just not the right way for things to pan out and so be blocking your angel from helping you. You're asking for the wrong path to the right result.

It's actually impossible for us to imagine the right way to get to where we want to be. It's too complicated, when you take into account the ripple effect. You just can't visualize the right path in detail, and by trying too hard to do so, you can change everything and make everything go wrong. So, leave that all up to your angel and just visualize the end result. And don't forget to always finish your request with the intent that things should happen 'for the highest possible good'.

Once you achieve your dream and look backwards with hindsight, you'll see a very detailed route map leading you to where you wanted to be. It will all make sense at this point, but before that you may well have wondered what on earth was going on and what your angels were thinking of, as they apparently led you away from your goal or down a path you never knew existed. By the time you reach your goal, though, you'll be able to see that although the path was twisty, it led to the right place.

To demonstrate how this works in reality, I'd like to share my and Tony's path in more detail.

I was allowed to sink into deep depression pretty much as a last resort, I believe, in order to be opened to a pathway I could never have imagined for myself. The pathway was to fulfilment, which was what I craved, though I didn't know how to get it. I'd gone down all kinds of dead ends in search of it, but they had brought me nothing but sadness and emptiness. And I wouldn't stay still long enough for my angel to help me. I didn't listen, I just kept running from project to project, searching for a reason to be alive, when all the time the answer was inside me.

At that point of deep depression I was finally open enough to hear my angel and I had my past-life awakening, which led me to start songwriting successfully and write my first book.

That awakening led me to want to travel to America (to meet my past-life soulmate) enough to overcome my lifelong fear of plane travel. Tony and I went to the USA and had our eyes opened by that amazing country (and by my past-life soulmate) to the possible joy of change. Up to that point we had both been too cautious to take any leaps of faith.

After that I convinced Tony to give up his very stressful, unrewarding job (which I am sure would have been the death of him by now had he stayed in it), sell our big house and land and move to the hills of the West Country.

Moving led me to start a whole new career in local television, which in turn led to greater publicity and mainstream radio guest slots and TV appearances, and from there to a publishing deal, on a small scale, and from there, eventually, to a major publishing deal for several books.

Being in a new place and seeing the changes in me led Tony to be open enough to try new therapies and train as a healer himself. His spiritual openness took him to a reflexology session with a woman who channelled as she worked and she told him that he should go for a prostate cancer test. He was also led to have the test administered directly by a nurse, whereas the usual protocol would be for a doctor to counsel him first about the possible downsides of being tested. If things had taken the conventional route and he'd seen the doctor first, the counselling might well have led to him talking himself out of the test.

When his results came back positive, the cancer was at such an early stage that he was able to stave it off for five years with diet and healing. His diet was dictated by Gwynne Davies, a clinical ecologist, and this led him to train as one himself. In this way he helped many sick people back to healthy lives. Because of his diet and self-healing abilities, when he finally did opt for surgery, his post-operative healing took half the expected time.

My own experiences gave me the strength to cope with this peril to my beloved husband in a way that I would have never dreamed possible. If this had happened a few years earlier, when I had no direct angelic support, I would certainly have folded under the stress.

I believe this change of lifestyle saved both our lives in the long run. I honestly doubt either of us would still be alive otherwise, because the dietary changes we made took me off the downhill spiral I was on and my health improved immensely.

All of the above, in one way or another, led me to achieve my life's ambition of earning a living as a writer, both of books and magazine columns, in a way that neatly fulfilled my life's purpose too – being a seed-planter. What better way was there for me to reach people and plant a seed of spirituality in their hearts than by writing about angels, past lives and spiritual matters in a way they could identify with?

SOME TIPS

Have Patience

As you can see, the pathways to the fulfilment of our desires can be very complex to arrange and so they take *time*. Don't expect big changes in a short time – that just can't happen in a successful and *right* way. We have to allow things to run at Heaven's schedule, not our own. So take comfort in small baby steps. As long as you continue to make them and get signs that things are changing, albeit slowly, then relax and *wait* with confidence.

This is one of the hardest things to learn and understand, but if you always finish your requests with the intent that things should happen 'for the highest possible good', you can be sure that you are on the right track.

Start Small

Start small with your angelic shopping list. Start with something that can be easily pictured, such as an item of jewellery, or a book or CD. Anything more esoteric, such as a message from a loved one, or anything bigger, such as a job promotion, can take practice.

'I'll see it when I believe it' is the way to success, rather than 'I'll believe it when I see it.' Once you've achieved a small item, your faith will increase, and so will your positive energy, and so will your ability to communicate with angels!

Above all, always finish your request with the intent that things should happen 'for the highest possible good'.

CHAPTER 8
ANGELIC VISITATIONS

There are many true accounts of angelic visitation throughout history and up to the present day. The Bible is full of accounts of heavenly beings bringing messages, and before that, the oldest recorded civilization, the Sumerians, carved statues of beings with wings. They called them 'messengers of the gods'. Descriptions of angels have changed greatly over the centuries and I believe this is because they have changed their appearance to suit the belief systems of humans.

Reading about amazing angelic encounters and other people's success at connecting with their angels might make you feel inadequate if you're not making much progress yet. But if you embrace all these accounts with joy in your heart, then you know by now what you'll create more of – positive energy! And from there, fraction by fraction, you'll be raising your vibration towards that of your angels, until one day, suddenly, you'll find yourself right there!

THE SHEPHERDS

The first account of angelic visions I'm going to give you here comes from the Bible and is the account of how shepherds in the fields were notified by an angel of the birth of Christ:

> *And behold, an angel of the Lord stood before them, and the glory of the Lord shone around them, and they were greatly afraid. Then the angel said to them, 'Do not be afraid, for behold, I bring you good tidings of great joy, which will be to all people. For there is born to you this day, in the city of David, a Saviour who is Christ the Lord.'*

Luke 2:9–11

THE GENTILE'S ANGEL

The Bible also tells us about Cornelius's encounter with an angel. Cornelius was a Roman centurion and a God-fearing man, and he was a Gentile, that is to say non-Jewish. One day he was praying when suddenly an angel appeared in front of him. He was, it is said, terrified at first. But the angel spoke to him and calmed him. He was told to find Peter. In the meantime, Peter was having his own angelic vision, telling him to go to Cornelius, which he did. So Cornelius was the first Gentile to be converted to Christianity. It was believed that his angelic vision provided proof that it was the will of God that Gentiles should be brought into the Church.

THE ANGEL AND THE SWORD

The Castel Sant'Angelo in Rome was so named because in the sixth century, during a time of plague, Pope Gregory was visited by an angel there. He is said to have seen the angel hovering above the building and placing its sword into a sheath. This vision heralded the end of the plague, and in honour of the angel a new sculpture of the archangel Michael was placed on the top of the building.

GEORGE WASHINGTON'S ANGEL

One of the most famous people to have claimed to have seen an angel was US President George Washington. During the American War of Independence, a soldier, Anthony Sherman, came across Washington looking very pale and shocked. When Sherman asked what the matter was, Washington said he'd just seen an angel. He made Sherman promise to keep the story a secret until after his death, but said that he'd been indoors, sitting at his desk and thinking deeply, when suddenly a bolt of unearthly light had shone into the room. When he'd turned to look for the source of the light he'd seen a very beautiful woman glowing all in silver, who had gone on to give him several predictions concerning the future of the United States.

These predictions were extremely lengthy and mostly dealt with warnings of perils to come, such as, 'Son of the Republic, look and learn.' Washington then saw a dark shadowy being, like an angel, floating in midair between Europe and America. Dipping water out of the ocean in the hollow of each hand, the angel sprinkled some upon America with his right hand, while with his left hand he cast some on Europe. Immediately a cloud rose up from these countries and joined in mid-ocean. For a while it remained stationary and then moved slowly westward until it enveloped America in its murky folds. Sharp flashes of lightning gleamed through it at intervals, and Washington claimed to have heard the smothered groans and cries of the American people.

It seems to me that this was a good representation of the Second World War.

THE ANGEL OF MONS

This is probably the best documented and most famous of angel visitations. It has stood the test of time because it was seen by many people. It took place in August 1914, at the start of the First World War, when the British Expeditionary Forces, who were vastly under-prepared, were outnumbered by German troops at Mons. The British troops were forced to retreat, leaving many dead and dying, helpless in the face of the enemy's advance. Several of the wounded soldiers were found later to have inexplicably been able to find their way back to safety, even though their wounds should have prevented it. They all claimed that angelic forms had descended from the sky and carried them to safety.

Many years have passed since this event and many sceptics have claimed the account of angels to be fantasy, but only the men who were there know for sure.

THE FATIMA ANGELS

In 1916 an angel appeared three times to three children, Lucia, aged nine, Francisco, aged eight, and Jacinta, aged six, at Fatima in Portugal. They were told that he was the Angel of Peace and that they need have no fear of him. He taught the children how to pray and told them that he had come to pave the way for an apparition of Our Lady. She did eventually appear to them a year later, on 13 May 1917, and then on the thirteenth of the month for the next eight consecutive months.

THE VATICAN ANGEL

In 2007 American news channels and newspapers around the world reported that a policeman on holiday in Rome had photographed what appeared to be an angel in St Peter's Basilica in the Vatican. The angelic shape hovered over the heads of the people there, glowing white.

THE MIRACLE ANGEL

This story made news all over the USA. It involved a 14-year-old girl called Chelsea, who contracted pneumonia. She had already had many other severe health issues during her lifetime, having suffered from hydrocephalus, which required a shunt in her skull and several shunt revisions, as well as life-threatening viruses and fluid retention that involved more than a week's hospitalization and three litres of liquid being drawn from her body.

Chelsea's whole family was buoyed up by their faith in God and prayed every day that Chelsea would survive her latest test. They were constantly asking their angels to bring a miracle because Chelsea was on life support and the prognosis was grave. Unfortunately, there was one setback after another. Chelsea faced pneumonia in her left lung, then in her right lung, then sepsis, blood clots, staph infections, E. coli, a collapsed lung and feeding problems.

A meeting was finally held to discuss what the next course of action should be. Should they take her off the ventilator? Her mother, Colleen, felt that she'd had her daughter for 14 years and had been blessed to have kept her for so long. So a decision was made – they'd take Chelsea off the ventilator and if God decided to take her then and there, they would accept it and let her go.

They took her off and at first she was able to breathe on her own and all seemed to be going well. But the next day she had to go back on an oxygen mask. For a few days nothing seemed to improve and Chelsea was finding it very hard to keep her spirits up.

Colleen said, 'She'd been through enough. I wanted to take her mask off. I wanted to do what the Lord wanted me to do. And I really felt that I'd had her for 14 years and if it was time for her to go to heaven, then I knew she'd be healed there.'

The family gathered to say what they thought would be their goodbyes to Chelsea. But a nurse took Colleen aside and showed her the closed-circuit TV monitor that was covering the door to the paediatric intensive-care unit.

'On the monitor, there was this bright light,' Colleen recalled, 'and I looked at it and I said, "Oh, my goodness! It looks like an angel!" The nurse said that in her 15 years at the hospital, she'd never seen anything like it.'

Colleen was able to take a photo of the image on the screen with her digital camera and says that photo gave her total peace that stayed with her as the oxygen mask was removed from Chelsea's face.

At that moment Chelsea's vital signs shot up. The doctors and nurses attending were all amazed by her good colour and responses.

Colleen believes that the angel was a sign that Chelsea would recover and that it had performed a miracle in answer to their prayers.

Of course angels often save children because their connection to their Guardian Angel is stronger than that of most adults, as mine was when I was a child. Sue, of Cheltenham in the UK, sent me this story:

My little boy Samuel was only eight months old. I was a paranoid mum and I can't explain how this accident was allowed to happen, but I suppose that's why they're called accidents! I'd been giving Samuel his breakfast in his high chair, right by the kitchen counter, well out of reach of the cooker, the kettle and anything else that seemed in any way dangerous, when the postman rang the doorbell. I went to get the package he couldn't fit through the letterbox and then hurried back to the kitchen. I must have only been gone a few seconds.

When I came back into the room, what I saw shocked and horrified me: Samuel was surrounded by bright electrical sparks and his little body was practically glowing. We figured out later that his daddy, Kel, had been fixing a loose cupboard hinge the night before and he'd left his screwdriver on the worktop. Then I'd put a magazine on top of it so we'd both missed seeing it there. Samuel had picked it up and shoved it into the electric plug socket on the wall. The worst thing was that the plastic handle had broken off the screwdriver shaft, so he was holding mostly metal.

Of course, when I saw him, I screamed. At that point Samuel must have dropped the screwdriver. My eyes were shut by then. I fully expected to open them and see my baby slumped in the high chair with smoke coming off his poor little body. But then I heard a chuckle. I opened my eyes and in disbelief I saw Samuel surrounded by a white light. It wasn't like a ball, but it was touching him all over, as if he was wearing a suit of silver.

As I rushed to him the silver suit faded and there was my little boy totally unhurt and giggling at me. I couldn't believe it! It seemed to me that Samuel's guardian angel had protected him with the silver suit.

THE 9/11 ANGELS

During the terrible tragedy of the terrorist attack on the World Trade Center Towers, many films were shot and many photos were taken. Some people claim there were many demonic faces in the smoke, but I honestly think you can make anything out of a photo of smoke if you try hard enough. But some people say they saw something different: angels flying up and out of the falling debris, carrying the souls of the dead in their arms. These are the people I believe.

There are those among us who believe that the terrible number of deaths that day created a necessary energy shift on the planet. They say that the souls who died offered themselves in this sacrifice for the world before they were born into this life, so of course they were carried aloft out of the pain and fear by their Guardian Angels. I like to think they are right.

CHAPTER 9
ANGELS AND CHILDREN

Children naturally see and talk to angels because they haven't been switched on to the material world. They only lose the ability as they grow up, become socially aware and start to feel self-conscious or worried about seeming odd and not fitting in. Conforming is very important to children and as the majority of them aren't encouraged to stay in touch with their angels, they don't do so, while the ones that are encouraged tend to push the angels away just to be one of the crowd.

Sadly, children are losing their angelic connection earlier and earlier in their lives. It's easy to see why. In this age of designer toys and designer clothes, children are bombarded with advertisements by the TV and magazines, so much so that their minds are turned towards material possessions at a much younger age than they used to be. Children used to have toys that stretched their imaginations, and I know that as a child I had very little interest in what I wore. But now, because of computer games that are virtual worlds, some children's imaginations have become stagnant.

This is devastating, because a child in a state of imaginative play is also in a state of meditation. When children playact they are open to a connection to their angels. When their minds are full of computer images, often featuring killing and violence, their imagination is sidelined and they become almost robotic. This is not like meditation; it's more like soul death. In this kind of state they are wide open to negativity.

We all want our children to have happy childhoods, to be popular and to feel good about themselves, but nowadays this has all got way out of control. Children have become mini-adults, dragged into a world that is rife with negativity, fear and a belief that the material world is all. Because of the pressure of conforming to their peers, they are fashion victims from an early age. Parents often struggle to meet their demands, because they feel that otherwise they'll be letting their kids down in some way and stopping them from fitting in. It's no wonder that the world has found itself deeper and deeper in trouble as whole generations have grown up like this.

Children are also bombarded now with Wi-Fi and mobile phone waves. I believe that this is pollution of the worst kind and in years to come we will greatly regret the installation of these devices in almost every municipal building. We are in danger, if nothing changes, of creating a spiritual wasteland in years to come.

Luckily, there is a counterbalance to all this. Some children are raised differently. Their parents know that kids who are 'different' often grow up to be the most innovative and valued members of society.

Standing up for a belief in the spiritual world should in fact be something we all strive for and it's something our children shouldn't be ashamed of. It's important to encourage your child or children not to lose their innate ability to connect with their angels as they grow up. Children are our race's future, and also the future of this planet, and if they are brought up to value and consider other life forms, however lowly, then both people and planet have a chance in the future. A child who is educated to realize that they are connected to, and dependent upon, every other living thing on the planet will never grow up to be a violent criminal. A child with an awareness of spirit will become a productive, progressive soul filled with white energy.

Spirituality of this kind is not about organized religions with all their associated man-made dogma, but that inner sense of connection to each other that we all should have and that prevents us from deliberately harming another living soul. Spirituality is an acknowledgement that we are not islands and our actions always affect others and our environment. Spirituality is a deep, intuitive connection to, and caring for, the place that we call Earth. It is an awareness that the important things to think of during our journey in our current bodies are not having the best house, car, furniture or holiday, or having the highest-paid job, but living for the good of our souls, which will be our essence long after our bodies have gone.

Without a spiritual grounding children can grow up to be vacant, damaged individuals who are inherently lonely and afraid. In these times, when talk of hunger, greed, war, terrorism, paedophilia and violent death is the norm, it is no wonder so many young people go completely off the rails in attempts to dull that fear and hopelessness with drugs and alcohol. It's a parent's job to make hope available to their child, together with knowledge that their inner light can affect that of the whole world and make change possible. So how it be done?

HOW CAN YOU MAINTAIN A CHILD'S SPIRITUALITY?

One of the first ways to open your child's eyes to the right way of being is by showing them how to handle pets and wild animals with compassion and understanding. Teach your children that animals have feelings that are just as valid as theirs are. Tell them that as caretakers of their pets they are responsible for the way those pets are made to feel. A child that has empathy with and respect for all other living creatures will grow to be an asset to the planet, a joy to their parents and a progressive spiritual being.

Children should also be taught to be considerate of others and not pollute their space with over-loud noise or litter. One way to be spiritual is to show respect, always, to all things.

Pay attention to your child and don't make fun of them if they speak of past lives or angels, or even invisible friends. Nurture their beliefs in the spiritual world so that they don't lose their angelic connection too young. Don't push the material worries of the world on them too early.

Like all other creatures, humans are still evolving, but in a spiritual rather than a physical direction. There are children being born today who are destined to lead the world into a new era. These children are called indigo or crystal children. They are recognized by their penetrating eyes, their wisdom, which is beyond their years, and their gentle and forgiving nature. They have innate psychic ability and with the right nurturing they will grow into powerful adults who will have a warrior spirit, one that will be capable of tearing down and rebuilding all the aspects of human life that have led us in the wrong direction, through politics, education and industry. These children are vitally important for the future of the human race and our home, the Earth. If you suspect you are the parent of such a child, then you have an even greater responsibility to encourage their naturally spiritual nature and develop any psychic gifts they might have. However, every child is special and every child born into these difficult times has an important role to play in our future.

Nowadays it's not that rare to see a disturbed child full of negative emotions, who has lost all connection to the spiritual world, turning on his classmates, committing random acts of violence and even using guns and knives to kill and maim. It worries me that the reasons behind these kinds of acts aren't investigated enough. These kids are bombarded with negative influences in the name of progress which unnaturally speed up their brainwaves, so why not take measures like sound therapy to counteract this with positive influences that will slow their brainwaves down? It would be a good idea if someone like Diane Egby-Edwards was invited into schools to use sound therapy on the children.

FEAR – THE OPPOSITE OF ANGELIC CONNECTION

It is of vital importance that children today are not brought up in fear. To fill a child's soul and mind with dread and hopelessness for the future is tantamount to child abuse. It tears them away from their souls.

There are many reading this who will recall the terror they went through in their own childhood during the Cold War, when parents spoke openly of impending doom and annihilation by atomic bombs. It's no wonder that such children, brought up believing that the world could not be changed and that war was the natural state to be in, failed to bring peace and tranquility to the world. It is up to us as adults now to ensure that we don't make the same mistake with our children.

Famine, war, climate damage – all these things can be changed by our children. They must believe that they have the power to make the world the way they want it to be, and then they will do so. That is why it is so vital that they are spiritual in nature and not selfish or cruel, and as parents we must do our utmost to make sure the right values are instilled in them from birth.

PAST LIVES

Children are always born with some knowledge of their past lives. They might manifest this by talking of 'previous mummies' or have 'invisible friends' who are actually their family or friends from a former lifetime. In some cases they might talk of their previous death or even be able to talk in a foreign language before they learn to speak the language of those around them.

Some parents are, naturally, totally freaked out by this kind of thing and immediately tell the child not to be silly. This belittlement and scorn can totally quash the child. An aware parent who wants to nurture spirituality in their child will do the opposite – encourage without pressure, keep notes for future reference and let their child know that it's a good and wonderful thing to maintain contact with their soul.

If your child has such memories, take them seriously and ask gentle questions. By asking about dates and details, it's easy to distinguish a real memory from make-believe. If the memories fade, as they often do at around the age of seven, when the child is old enough and ready you will have all the notes of your conversations there to remind them of who they once were and to show them that there's so much more to them than the envelope of their physical being.

ANGEL GRIDS

Angels are particularly attached to children and willing to protect and comfort them, and in fearful times their presence is essential to keep the child feeling safe and protected.

If, despite your care, your child is plagued by nightmares and night fears, help them make a crystal grid to call in their Guardian Angel at night. Let the child choose eight crystals and place them in a grid pattern. One should be the 'king' in the centre of a circle made up of the other seven. The most effective way to arrange them is to wire them to a copper base using copper wire, but any method will work.

Explain to your child that they have a Guardian Angel that they can rely on, one that can banish all the creatures of their nightmares and keep them safe while they sleep, and all they have to do is to look at the grid as they drift off and summon them. This way, your child will be able to go into a peaceful sleep each night and their vibration will become naturally high enough to easily communicate through the night with their angel.

One little girl, Sophie of New York, aged seven, had a very unusual angelic encounter. Her mother, Corinne, told me all about it:

Sophie's dad had been killed in a terrible road accident and she was very sad, but also very scared. She missed her dad terribly, and she especially missed the stories he used to read her at bedtime. These stories took away her fears of the day. Her favourite story was the one about a unicorn who came and took a sad little girl away to a magic land. The little girl had thought her parents didn't love her. She stayed in the magic land until she learned how much her parents had really loved her after all. Sophie had always been sad for the little girl and thought how lucky she was that she knew her mom and dad both loved her. Now she was worse off than the little girl in the book, because she didn't have a daddy at all.

A few days later Sophie heard me talking on the phone to my sister and telling her that there wasn't enough money and that I didn't know how I was going to cope. This scared her because she knew how much everything cost.

She was still in touch with her angel, and every night I watched her praying to him and smiled because I didn't believe in angels myself anymore and I thought it was cute that Sophie did.

One night Sophie went to sleep and dreamed of a unicorn that came and took her for a ride. Just like in the story, the unicorn could fly and he took Sophie way up into the sky. She could see the whole world stretched out below her and for a while she didn't feel sad or scared.

After a while she could see someone down on the ground. The unicorn flew lower and Sophie could see it was her dad.

The unicorn landed and Sophie ran into her dad's arms. He hugged her for a while and then he told her it was time for her to leave. She didn't want to go, but her dad told her that her angel was waiting to take her back. Sophie looked around in amazement at the unicorn, and realized it was really an angel. She could tell by the way it glowed.

She still didn't want to leave her dad, but he said she had to. He kissed her and told her there was an important message she had to take to her mom. He said he'd tried to tell her himself, but she couldn't hear him. He told her stuff that Sophie didn't really understand, but the main thing was that she had to make her mom check the bottom drawer of Dad's desk.

The next morning Sophie could remember her whole dream. She didn't tell me about the angel unicorn at the time, because she knew I wouldn't believe it, but she went to her dad's desk and looked in the bottom drawer. There was just one big brown envelope there. She brought it to me and, not knowing what to say, just held it out to me.

'What's this, honey?' I asked.

Sophie didn't answer. I shrugged and opened it. As I read the papers inside, my face lit up with a smile. I grabbed Sophie up and swung her round the room.

After several confusing visits from aunties, the whole story came out and Sophie understood what had happened. Her dad had taken out a life insurance policy before he died, but he hadn't had time to tell me about it. There was going to be plenty of money after all.

Of course, all the aunties wanted to know how Sophie had found the papers, so she told them. They told me, so I think they got the whole message, and I think now they are believers!

CHAPTER 10
ANGELS AND ANIMALS

Do animals have angels too? People sometimes say to me that there is no mention of them having souls or going to Heaven in the Bible. But that isn't surprising and doesn't mean they don't. After all, the Bible is a sort of instruction manual for humans to follow to reach Heaven and a pet or other animal wouldn't be able to go to Heaven through anything its owner could do, so why would there be any instructions about it in the human manual? But animals will be in Heaven anyway. If you doubt it, try to imagine Heaven with no animals in it. It's impossible.

THE CHARACTER OF ANIMALS VERSUS PEOPLE

When we look at the character of animals, it compares rather favourably with that of people…

Animals don't play emotional games; they're not Machiavellian and are incapable of deliberate manipulation by emotional blackmail.

Animal parents don't tolerate obnoxious or loutish behaviour from their young and therefore they don't place the blame elsewhere when it comes to producing unruly offspring. Young animals don't have tantrums or cause malicious damage and they don't disobey their parents.

Animals don't collect material possessions or feel a need to outdo their neighbours by demonstrably owning more or better items than they do.

As long as there is enough food and water to go around, animals will happily share. In times of plenty natural prey and predator combinations such as zebra and lion can be seen drinking side by side at waterholes. There is a crocodile-infested reservoir in Ghodahada, India, where cows and calves graze fearlessly in the meadows next to the water and people bathe from the banks. To this day, no cow or human, or their pets, has ever been attacked by the 13-foot reptiles. Even though the reservoir is fished regularly, the crocodiles have never attacked the fishermen. A scientific study put this down to fact that the humans don't interfere with the crocodiles and there is enough fish for everyone.

Animals are immensely forgiving and don't hold grudges, and best of all, they are in tune with the planet they live on. Left to their own devices, without interference from man, they would naturally keep in perfect balance with the Earth and keep the Earth itself in total balance.

Some people say that animals sometimes behave with bestiality and apparent cruelty, but they are comprised of many layers, as are humans. They are spirit, animal, species, breed (especially those who reproduction has been manipulated by humans) and finally personality. Those layers sometimes stifle the light of the spirit. Also, of course some animal souls, as with people, are less advanced than others because they've been here fewer times and haven't learned to stifle their baser personalities.

Animals are here to experience situations and emotions that can only be experienced within the envelope of their body, in the same way that humans are, and this includes their darker emotions. But their spirits sometimes shine more brightly than ours and that is because they are not here to experience the baser human emotions, such as greed, lust and taking pleasure from killing, kidnapping and using others. Likewise they are not equipped to manipulate others of their race in order to gain monetary wealth or power in the world.

I believe that one of the purposes of souls taking on physical bodies, whether human or animal, is to rise to a challenge. That challenge is to reunite the mind and body with the soul after being born in a way that tears these elements apart. Because animals are more naturally in tune with their intuition and don't have to overcome the human condition, which is beset by psychological barriers and materialistic tendencies, they have an easier task than we do.

FRAGMENTED SOULS

I am totally convinced that pets have souls and so are immortal. And to me, any living creature that is immortal must have a Guardian Angel or a connection to angels of some sort, so yes, I believe pets do have angels. I also believe in progressive reincarnation – that is, that our souls spend a lot of time in 'lower' life forms, which are our training ground for the most difficult phase spiritually, that of being human. I believe that during the progression through the lower life forms, i.e. insects, fish, reptiles, small mammals, birds, etc., only a part of a soul incarnates and that gradually, as it progresses up the 'thought chain', the soul fragments meld together until a whole soul is created in each of the higher life forms, such as large and/or domesticated mammals. So I believe that the lower life forms don't have an angel each, but that one angel takes care of a whole flock, herd, shoal or swarm. Also, it makes sense that if animals reincarnate, as I am convinced they do, angels are assigned to them to take care of that progression.

However, I don't believe animals need their angels in quite the same way as we do. This is because they still have the ability to live in the moment, which also means accepting what is, letting go of what has gone and not projecting into the future. We still have this ability when we first move into human form. As babies and children, it's natural for us to live in the moment. As we grow older and start to understand the gravity of being human, though, we lose it.

ANIMALS CARING FOR EACH OTHER

It seems to me that some animals are progressing spiritually more quickly than we are, and this may be because they are to be our future leaders when their souls take on a human body, our wise helpers in times of trouble. Recently, there has been more and more evidence of this. I've found many verifiable stories about how animals of different species are starting to take care of each other. And they are doing this while humankind is still having trouble getting along just because of different colours, different religions or different sexual preferences. Moreover, animals are not only looking after those of a different species, but they are often also doing it in classic hunter/prey combinations.

Cats and birds, for instance, are natural enemies, but in Massachusetts in the USA a couple was filming their garden when they saw a young kitten wandering around on its own. They were kind-hearted people and worried how the kitten, which was only a few months old, would survive without help. But as they filmed, something amazing happened: a crow came hopping up to it and started to feed it. It would go and get a worm or an insect and bring it back for the kitten, which would eat it. Not only that, but over the next few days they saw the crow playing with the kitten and guiding it to safety when it strayed into the road. The couple adopted the kitten and it slept in the house every night, but every morning the crow would be outside, waiting for it.

There are also several accounts of husky dogs making friends with and playing with polar bears – two more natural enemies.

In the aftermath of a hurricane a tiger cub was left an orphan. She was adopted by a chimpanzee who took over all the maternal duties, including bottle-feeding the cub.

In Kenya a baby hippo was rescued from the sea after losing its parents. The whole hippo family had been washed out to sea during the chaos of a tsunami and the baby had been left behind. The staff of the sanctuary that saved it were worried because they had no other hippos to befriend the baby. However, they soon discovered that the hippo had adopted a giant tortoise as its surrogate mother and the two of them were inseparable, even sleeping together, with baby hippo resting his head on the shell of the tortoise. The fact that the tortoise was 130 years old and the hippo only a baby further demonstrates the non-biased attitude of animals compared to that of humans.

On 4 December 2008 an amazing story was captured on a motorway camera in Santiago in Chile. At first sight the film looked as though it was going to be just another tragic road-victim tale, as a dog ran across the carriageways. Appearing to be in a blind panic, it paid no attention to the speeding traffic and the inevitable soon happened: it was struck a glancing blow by two cars and was left sprawled unconscious and obviously badly injured or dead, right in the middle of the carriageway.

It looked as if the dog was soon to become a smear on the tarmac, reduced from a living, breathing creature to a greasy stain. But then on the edge of the camera's range, another dog appeared. It looked very similar to the other one, so you have to wonder if they were siblings. The second dog paused for a moment as if assessing the problem and then carefully made his way across the lanes of traffic to the prone dog. At this point, for me, it became quite surreal, as the rescuer dog didn't grasp the injured one with his mouth, the way you would expect a dog to, but instead put a front leg either side of the victim from the front, his paws under the armpits, as you would see a human do when attempting to drag a heavy person. Then the dog, step by painstaking step, walked backwards across the motorway, looking carefully at the traffic each time it crossed a lane, avoiding the speeding cars and dragging its friend along until it reached the safety of the central reservation.

Sadly, there wasn't a really happy ending, as the first dog had died on impact and its rescuer ran away before motorway workers, running to the scene to help, could take it in to be homed.

But there are many things to consider in this story. How was the second dog able to assess the situation so intelligently? If it was just a 'dumb animal', how did it know that its friend needed rescuing? If it was incapable of love, then why would it care anyway? It was obviously very clever to be able to make it unscathed onto, across and off the three-lane road, but when it reached the other dog, it must have been able to sense that it was too late to save its life and yet something drove it to still want its friend's body off the road. Why would a dog care what happened to a dead body and pull it so laboriously off the road instead of just saving itself? Did it want its friend's body to be respected? If so, this is hardly the thought process of an irrational mind. Why did it use the totally human way of dragging the other dog, instead of grasping it with its teeth, which would have made its journey back much safer and quicker? Over and above all these remarkable questions, the biggest one of all remains: why did it embark on the rescue in the first place? There can only be one answer: it loved the other dog.

These animals certainly have souls and that being the case they must also have angels. I believe I once experienced a direct connection between my Guardian Angel and the angel watching over a pair of dogs. This happened within about five miles of my home. Tony and I were driving down one of those fast country lanes that people seem to use as a racetrack. It was pretty straight along most of its length, but there were one or two blind bends. I was driving and as I neared a bend I heard the instruction I've had before to slow down. Of course I obeyed and soon I saw why, as running around the bend towards us came two loose dogs. One was a Labrador and the other a Border terrier. They ran past our car and it wasn't going to take more than a few seconds for them to get mown down by the next one.

I stopped the car and we jumped out. The two dogs kept running in the opposite direction, ignoring us, panic on their faces. I said to my Guardian Angel, 'Please talk to their angel and have him tell them to trust me.'

'Hey, boys! Where you going?' I called out.

Both dogs stopped instantly, turned around and ran right to me. One of them was wearing a collar with a telephone number on it. The code was for a town about six miles away.

I called the number on my mobile phone. A young girl answered and told me her mum was out looking for the dogs and didn't have a phone with her. So we were a bit stuck. We couldn't possibly leave the dogs and we couldn't fit them into our car and we had no way of knowing where their frantic owner was or of guiding her to us. Again I asked my angel to help us. Specifically I asked that the owner be guided to us.

Literally a minute later a car sped along the road and tooted its horn the moment the driver saw us. She overtook us, stopped her car and came running back to us. It was the dogs' owner and they were overjoyed to see her. She was very grateful to us for helping her dogs, but really she should have been grateful to our angels.

ANIMAL ANGELS

I would go a step further than saying animals have angels: I believe that sometimes animals *are* angels, or at least that for a certain period of their lives they can play host to an angel within their bodies. This accounts for the way that they tend to arrive at the exactly right time and in exactly the right place to be of the most benefit to their owners. I know that some animals go wrong, but when they do, particularly in the example of pet dogs that bite people, there is always a human fault behind it. Dogs would naturally live an ordered life with no conflict in the pack. When unpredictable, dis-ordered humans become the dog's pack, things can become unbalanced because the humans are, and this leads to unbalanced and possibly aggressive dogs.

Generally, dogs happily give their lives to service, often helping their blind, deaf or disabled owners to live a much more normal life than they could alone. Monkeys, too, are trained to assist disabled people. Pets so often come into a person's life at just the right moment to help them through a difficult time. Animals even have the ability to rehabilitate young offenders and to show them, maybe for the first time, that there is love in the world. They couldn't do all the good they do without being strongly connected to the divine, and sometimes even *being* the divine. I believe that animals will play a huge part in the changes that are to come for all of us.

Sometimes an angel can be sent to Earth in a small dog's body to save someone special. This story was reported by news teams all over the world. It is about a baby boy born to a 14-year-old girl in a shanty town, just outside Buenos Aires. The young mother panicked when the baby was born and abandoned him in a field, surrounded by stacks of rubbish and old wooden crates. No one would have heard him crying in the remote spot where he was left. He would have died quite quickly if not for the actions of an angel in the body of a dog.

La China, an eight-year-old dog who had puppies of her own at the time, found the baby, picked him up and carried him gently in her mouth, taking him across a road and through fences to eventually place him alongside her own puppies. Now within hearing, the baby was heard crying by La China's owner, who called the police. The little boy, weighing 8lb 13oz, had some slight injuries, but no bite marks at all, as La China had only grabbed him by the rags he was wrapped in, and he was eventually taken to the authorities.

Who knows what kind of man this baby will grow up to be and what amazing things he might accomplish? It's obvious that he was meant to live and that his angels took steps to make sure he did.

This final animal angel story comes from Andy Reeve, from Cornwall in the UK, and is about his angel cat Tilly:

I do three night shifts a week and one morning I arrived home a little after 6 a.m. I had breakfast, etc., and went to bed. Two hours later I woke to find that Tilly was sitting on my chest, quite literally poking me in the eye. I was rather cross at first, but then I quickly discovered that the entire flat was full of gas. It seems that I must have nudged a gas tap on the cooker to the 'on' position during breakfast, but hadn't lit it.

A couple of things occurred to me later. I had an old central heating boiler then with a pilot light burning merrily away. The next few minutes could have seen an explosion that could have killed all the people in the entire block, as well as Tilly. She herself obviously didn't know this (but perhaps the angel that took up temporary residence in her did) and she could have just said to herself, 'I don't like this smell. I'm out of here!' and legged it through the cat door. But (thank you, Universe), she didn't.

Thank the universe or thank the angel?

CHAPTER 11

CREATING AN ANGEL SANCTUARY

By now you'll be starting to accept the presence and communication of your angels, and you should understand that angels can come to you anywhere, at any time, but it's still a very good idea to create a special place in your home and, if you have one, in your garden too. Using this place will help to give your mind the inner peace it will need in order to hear your angels. The place itself will start to be a trigger so that you'll be halfway towards the right state without really trying.

If you can dedicate a private area to it, all the better, but if not, a quiet corner will do. This is somewhere you can go and sit whenever you're feeling a bit stressed out and in need of a serious angel 'hug', or you're preparing yourself for some deep meditation, or you want to ask your Guardian Angel for something. It would also be a very good place to write your angel shopping list, or to ask your angel its name if you haven't already got it. Just the idea of being in a designated place for angel communication can be very helpful. And if you're getting a little impatient while waiting for help from your angel, it's also a good place to sit and ask your angel to very kindly 'get a move on' if they can!

It's not a bad idea to also select a special time for your ritual. As with any mediation, prepare yourself and your site by making sure pets are out of the way and you won't be disturbed by the kids arriving from school or a partner coming in from work. In fact it's quite nice to time using your sanctuary so that you'll be finished not long before the family arrives home. That way they'll always find you calm, receptive and ready to give them your time. And as energy, good or bad, travels, you may well find that your emotional stability will rub off on them and you'll all have a more pleasant time together because of it.

INDOORS
Choosing your Space
One good place to put your sanctuary would be in the bathroom. Relaxing in a hot bath at the same time as communing with your angels can only help the connection. Add to this the fact that water is a very sacred and vital part of the universe and you can see why angels and water go together beautifully.

Preparing your Sanctuary
Start with a focus point. This can be a piece of angel artwork, a Buddha statue, a beautiful violet-coloured flower or anything that feels right.

Around this you should place some crystals and candles. The table on which they stand should be covered if possible in pastel-coloured natural fabrics, such as silk. Try to avoid nylon or anything man-made. Hemp or cotton would be better than polyester or the like.

When choosing the colours of the candles and cloths and crystals, bear in mind the angelic colours are violets, mauves, purples and pinks.

Make a crystal wand to place there too. Buying these ready-made can be horrendously expensive, but you can make one with a nice quartz crystal and a piece of driftwood. It can be fun and uplifting to scour the beaches for a piece with a convenient hole in it to fit the crystal into. Some glass glue and a good imagination will also be required.

Try and get some stained-glass angels to hang in and around your sanctuary. In these beautiful ornaments you have a combination of the power of the symbolic angel, light and colour, so you really can't go wrong.

Have some big floor cushions ready to bring to the sanctuary to sit on.

It's also good to bring fire, in some form, into your angel sanctuary. Fire, when used safely of course, is very good at generating positive energy. On a cold day you can see how everyone is warmed immediately just by the sight of an open fire. An open fire relaxes you and staring into a flame can take you into a meditative state without really trying. What can you do if you haven't got an open fire? Fortunately there are things called fire bowls, usually made of copper or occasionally ceramics, that can be filled with a substance called fire gel. A lit fire bowl can be almost as atmospheric as an open log fire and it doesn't require a chimney. The colours of the fire-bowl flames are orange, just like those of an open fire. If a fire bowl isn't available, you can use candles as your fire, though candle flames, while better than nothing, tend to be a bit dazzling and yellow.

IN THE GARDEN
Choosing your Space
You can place your angel sanctuary anywhere in your garden that feels right to you, but do make sure you have something nice to sit on, such as a big flat rock or a wooden stool. Natural materials are best. No plastic!

If you can manage it, it's a good idea to curtain off your area with voile curtains suspended from poles, a bit like a four-poster bed. If you have a summerhouse, you can create your sanctuary inside it, which means you won't have to take down the curtains in winter.

Preparing your Sanctuary
Have some water in your sanctuary, even if it's just a shallow bowl. Running water is best if you can manage it. The sound of water is very soothing and calming, so it makes a good aid to meditation. Don't have fish in your water feature, though, as their energy can interfere with yours.

Make it a bit of a hobby to buy lovely big stones every time you visit a garden centre, as anything natural and beautiful will enhance the space.

Your garden sanctuary can also benefit from crystals. Water and crystals go very well together – after all, water itself has a crystalline structure and it represents one of the four elements. Really use your imagination for the other elements. Maybe make a circle of red stones, such as jasper (for angel communication) to signify fire. Hang some blue stones, such as kyanite (emotional support) from a home-made mobile to represent the air or sky, and stack a heap of sunstone (which cleanses your chakras) to represent the earth. Have one element at each corner of your sanctuary and finally choose a very special stone as the guardian of your sanctuary, such as bloodstone, which will protect and define the space.

Incidentally, clear quartz buried in the soil next to an ailing plant will work wonders.

Candles are always a good addition to an outdoor sanctuary, as are mirrors. Fire bowls work just as well outside as in and are a good way of bringing the warmth of real flames into your garden sanctuary too.

My ideal version of an angel sanctuary in the garden would be made by using all of the above, but putting it inside a tree house. I have a special empathy with trees and I think the marrying of angels and trees would be just about as perfect a union as could be. If you haven't got a tree house, then you wouldn't go far wrong by creating your sanctuary in the shade of a suitable tree.

Using silk and curtains and candles and mirrors and stained-glass angels might seem a bit self-indulgent, but feeling pampered creates endorphins, and endorphins create positive energy, and positive energy creates higher vibrations, so go for it! These sanctuaries are all about making you feel good.

USING YOUR SANCTUARY

Before you enter your sanctuary, wherever it may be, take a little time to centre yourself and make sure you don't take any negative energy in with you. If you've had to be out in the world and think you may have picked up some negative energy from those around you, drink some crystal elixir to clear it.

State your intention before entering the sanctuary and after a few deep breaths you'll be ready.

LEY LINES

It's always a good idea to check out the location of your home with regard to ley lines and other forms of earth energy. Ley lines are naturally occurring magnetic energy lines that run all around the planet. They sometimes form vortexes of energy that can affect the growth of plants and trees. In Sedona in Arizona, among the sculpted red rocks of this amazingly spiritual place, the juniper trees have spirally twisted branches caused by the energy vortexes.

The magnetic energy that ley lines generate can be capitalized on with the use of crystal grid mandalas. These are a selection of crystals wired to a copper board, similar to the ones I suggested to help children sleep well. The mandala should be placed in the ground to allow benevolent energy to be collected from the ley lines.

When I was creating my own sanctuaries in different houses I encountered a couple of slightly unusual problems that some of you might also experience. The house I am in now turned out to have been built at the very centre of a straight line between two Bronze Age barrows. These are ancient burial sites. This meant that we had a lot of disturbances caused by physic energy, as spirits were using what was to them a natural highway. The answer was simple: the spirits had to be contacted and gently encouraged to go 'to the light'. They were guided there by my angel. We have to repeat the procedure every now and then.

In another house, we were conscious of having negative energy leaking in. We thought it was coming from a neighbour's house. I had to ask my angels to erect a light barrier between us and our neighbours, who didn't mean any harm, but were inadvertently sending negative thought patterns in our direction.

I thought it was solved, but then felt some more energy travelling under my feet. Tony remembered that our fireplace had an underfloor draught tunnel, and once that was closed and glass fire doors fitted in front of the fireplace, all was well.

If you feel you may have disturbances in your house, your angel might be able to help, but if they are caused by someone else, remember your angel can't influence other people or their energies. If this is the case you'll need to find a professional, as I did.

AFTERWORD

Here are some little quick tips and wrinkles on how to get your angel to protect you every day and create a positive life at home and away. This is turn will raise your vibrations and bring you ever closer to your angels.

- Perform 'random acts of kindness'. Doing something nice for someone without reason or reward does wonders for your own energy. It creates endorphins and this of course creates positive energy. Angels warm to this kind of thing and of course it's good for your karma in future lives too.

- Bless your food before you eat or drink it. The custom of saying grace before meals has all but died out and in fact a lot of families never sit down to eat together at all. Saying grace is not just an outdated tradition – saying positive words over your food has a scientifically proven effect on its molecules. A Japanese researcher, Masaru Emoto, performed experiments which entailed putting labels onto bottles of water. The water's molecular structure changed according to the emotions of the words on that particular bottle. They became more structured and balanced with positive words, and disrupted and unbalanced by negative words. You'll even get more nourishment from your food and water if you bless it and imbue it with positive emotions! Try and eat blessed meals together as a family at least once a week and make a positive energy-laden ritual of it.

- Never sit down to eat while allowing negativity to enter your food. For instance, never eat while watching the news on TV or reading the paper. Refuse to discuss disharmonious issues, money worries or health concerns while eating. Even if only for that short time, limit your talk to anything good that happened or that you heard about throughout the day.

- Don't pass on bad news. We all play a part in creating our own reality, and indeed that of the planet. Focusing on or discussing or even thinking about gloomy things can be interpreted as a wish to create them. So do be careful what you wish for – even if you don't mean to wish for it!

- Have an honesty circle. This means at least once a week the whole family sits in a circle, facing outwards and holding hands. Each person must take a turn in saying with complete honesty and openness how the family has made them feel emotionally during the preceding week, both good and bad. Anything said in this circle remains in the circle and no one is ever punished for their honesty.

- Cleanse your house every now and then with crystals, singing bowls or smudging. This should always be done on moving into a new home to clear away any negative energy from the previous occupants. If the previous occupants had a lot of arguments, for instance, the energy from those arguments can linger in the house. The same thing applies if *your* family is trying to sell a house that has had a lot of discord in it – people may sense it and not buy! So, if this is the case, make sure you cleanse the house every time a potential buyer is going to call.

- Don't ever judge yourself harshly, because your angels won't. Guilt is one of the most useless and damaging emotional states to hang onto. It's often spawned from a past-life experience and is never something that should compromise your current life or block you from connecting to your angels.

- Keep a pad and pen by the bed because once you get an angelic connection you never know when a message might come through. Sometimes messages are so amazing that even in your befuddled state of half-waking you'll think there's no way that you'll have forgotten them when you wake up – but you will. When the messages come through, your mind is in an altered state and when you wake up it isn't. I have lost count of the number of times I have been shown something amazing in the middle of the night, something that has filled me with a sense of wonder, and yet in the light of day I have no recollection of what it was. It's *so* frustrating! So have the pen and paper ready so that you can sit up and write the information down.

- Have an aura photo taken of each family member and decorate their rooms to match their auras. This empowers their energy in their own rooms, which should always be a sanctuary for them. Try and make the main living room, or any shared rooms, a balanced blend of everyone's aura, so long as the colours don't clash too much. If they do, then just add tiny splashes of the colours that 'don't go'.

- First thing in the morning, 'clothe' each family member in your mind's eye in a silver suit of protection. This will help to empower your and their angels to provide protection during the day and prevent unnecessary accidents happening.

- Form a bubble of the same material over the house each morning and each night. This will discourage unwanted callers and even stop burglars finding your home an attractive proposition.

- If you're travelling in a car, envelop it in white or silver light. You'll note that tail-gaters pull back when you push the bubble towards their car. This can be especially helpful on motorways, where drivers often tend to drive too close to the car in front. This energy bubble will also prevent anyone getting angry with you or your driving and stop 'road rage' happening to you.

- If at all possible, invest in some stained glass somewhere in the house, preferably in a south-facing room. The multiple colours will bring light and healing into the house. We often underestimate the power of light and colour, but our angels know that we need this kind of energetic stimulation. That's why they usually appear to us as bright colours and lights.

- Nutritionists will tell you that 'you are what you eat', and it's true, because our cells can only be regenerated using the material that we feed them. I'd like you to consider the same thing about your energy. In other words, your energy is made up largely of the information you consume. In the world we live in at the moment, we're bombarded by negative information. News items, often embellished to make them more sensational, constantly push negative emotions through us. That's why it's so important not only to avoid thinking and talking about negative issues as much as possible but also to establish a deep inner core of positivity. Without its stability, communication with your angels will just fade away. So all the methods I've shown you in this book must be kept up.

My last word is one of the most important to me. While angels are not like Tinkerbell in that one dies if someone says they don't believe in them, there are some very good reasons why we need more people to believe in them. Every person on the planet, enlightened or not, a believer or not, spiritual or not, good or bad, knows that this world is in serious trouble and that we need help. A lot of people are aware of the Mayan Calendar that prophesizes an 'ending' in the year 2012 and some are worried that it means the end of the world. It doesn't. Angels have told me that there is an 'ending' planned, but not one that you might fear. It is planned that there will be an end to suffering, an end to greed, an end to fighting, an end to the rat race, an end to material wealth, an end to starvation, an end to disease and an end to fear, and that the world we know and all its people will change.

This sounds wonderful, but we have to achieve perfect balance by then. That might sound impossible, but in order to achieve that balance we actually only need to achieve critical mass. The angels will do the rest. What critical mass means is that enough people must become enlightened to 'tip the scales' or 'throw the switch'. If that switch is thrown, then at that moment every single soul on the planet will be instantly enlightened and the change will occur.

Critical mass can be demonstrated by comparing the energy of the Earth to a huge glass of water. At this moment in time the water/energy would be pretty cloudy and dirty with negativity. But imagine that we can each pour our own energy-filled glass into the world's glass and that if we try hard enough we can make our water so pure and positive that it will have the same effect as tipping bleach into dirty water. With each pure glass that is poured in, the clarity of the planet's energy will be improved, until, if enough bleach is poured in, its water will become totally clear.

So, if you ever think you don't count or that you aren't important, think again. Every time you mention an angel, or find an angel mentioned, whether it be on TV or in a conversation or in a magazine, that is another tiny, tiny step towards critical mass. If you have the courage to speak of angels and to admit to believing in them, even in the face of ridicule, you are contributing to critical mass. If one soul who hears about you talking to angels starts to open to the possibility of believing in them, then that is one more step towards critical mass.

If we don't achieve critical mass, then all that will happen is that the world will carry on as before – but that isn't a desirable outcome for any of us.

So have courage and go forward – gently. Angels don't want us to start driving dogmatic beliefs down people's throats. That would be counterproductive. They just want all you angel lovers out there to be open and honest about saying that you believe they are real and to tell your story. *They will do the rest.*

RESOURCES

Video Footage

Cat and crow: http://uk.youtube.com/
watch?v=1JiJzqXxgxo

Dog on motorway: http://www.youtube.com/
watch?v=PgWUeI3AHrs

Therapies, Readings and Reviews

- Angel Energy Healing: www.anexchangeoflove.
com

- Quantum Angel Healing®: http://www.
quantumangel.com/index.htm

- Angel Therapy: http://www.angeltherapy.com/

- Chelsea's angel photo: http://www.thestate.com/
breaking/story/629997.html

- Angel Touch Reiki: http://www.tranquiljourney.
co.uk

- Soul Angel readings: www.pastlifehelp.co.uk

- Janet Boyer: www.JanetBoyer.com (author of *The
Back in Time Tarot Book*)

- Channelled angel readings: http://www.solana. co.uk

- Angel portraits: http://www.patrickgamble.com/

- Sound therapy: Diane Egby-Edwards: http:// degby.wetpaint.com/

Books

- Ishvara d'Angelo, *Angels in our Time*, O Books, 2006

- Jan de Avalon, *Modern Angel Magic*, O Books, 2008

- Lorna Fitzgerald Byrne, *Angels in my Hair*, Century, 2008

- Judy Hall, *The Encyclopedia of Crystals*, Fair Winds Press, 2007

- Jacky Newcomb, *Angel by my Side*, HarperElement, 2006

- Jenny Smedley, *Souls Don't Lie*, O Books, 2006. My own past-life experience.

- Doreen Virtue, *Healing with the Angels*, Hay House, 1999

- Richard Webster, *Spirit Guides and Angel Guardians*, Llewellyn Publications, 1998

Angel Specialists

- Jacky Newcomb: www.jackynewcomb.co.uk

- Doreen Virtue: www.angeltherapy.com

Other

- The Barefoot Doctor – positivity: http://www.barefootdoctorglobal.com/

- Crystal elixirs: http://hubpages.com/hub/Making-Crystal-Elixiers

- Crystal mandalas: http://www.ablentrust.com/crystalmand.htm

- Near-death studies and support: Rev. Juliet Nightingale: www.TowardTheLight.org

- Andy Reeve: http://www.aardvarkrecords.co.uk

- Stained-glass angels: www.acornstainedglass.com

- Water experiments: http://www.masaru-emoto.net/english/entop.html

Love is a circle that never ends. Hate is a snake that consumes itself.

Jenny Smedley

ABOUT THE AUTHOR

Based in beautiful Somerset in the UK and happily married for 40 years, Jenny Smedley is an author, television and radio presenter/guest, international columnist and spiritual consultant specializing in past lives and angels. She is an animal intuitive and tree communicator. Her own current life was turned around by a vision from one of her past lives, and problems and issues related to that life were healed and resolved in a few seconds.

Jenny has appeared on many television shows and hundreds of radio shows around the world, including the UK, USA, Australia, New Zealand, Iceland, Tasmania, the Caribbean, South Africa and Spain.

After being shown her Master Path by an angel, Jenny was given the ability to create Mirror Angel portraits and to help others connect to their angels. Her website is: www.jennysmedley.com.

© Tony Smedley

NOTES

NOTES

We hope you enjoyed this Hay House book.
If you would like to receive a free catalogue featuring additional
Hay House books and products, or if you would like information
about the Hay Foundation, please contact:

Hay House UK Ltd
292B Kensal Road • London W10 5BE
Tel: (44) 20 8962 1230; Fax: (44) 20 8962 1239
www.hayhouse.co.uk

***

Published and distributed in the United States of America by:
Hay House, Inc. • PO Box 5100 • Carlsbad, CA 92018-5100
Tel: (1) 760 431 7695 or (1) 800 654 5126;
Fax: (1) 760 431 6948 or (1) 800 650 5115
www.hayhouse.com

***

Published and distributed in Australia by:
Hay House Australia Ltd • 18/36 Ralph Street • Alexandria, NSW 2015
Tel: (61) 2 9669 4299, Fax: (61) 2 9669 4144
www.hayhouse.com.au

***

Published and distributed in the Republic of South Africa by:
Hay House SA (Pty) Ltd • PO Box 990 • Witkoppen 2068
Tel/Fax: (27) 11 467 8904
www.hayhouse.co.za

***

Published and distributed in India by:
Hay House Publishers India • Muskaan Complex • Plot No.3
B-2• Vasant Kunj • New Delhi - 110 070
Tel: (91) 11 41761620; Fax: (91) 11 41761630
www.hayhouse.co.in

***

Distributed in Canada by:
Raincoast • 9050 Shaughnessy St • Vancouver, BC V6P 6E5
Tel: (1) 604 323 7100
Fax: (1) 604 323 2600

***

Sign up via the Hay House UK website to receive the Hay House
online newsletter and stay informed about what's going on with your
favourite authors. You'll receive bimonthly announcements
about discounts and offers, special events, product highlights,
free excerpts, giveaways, and more!
www.hayhouse.co.uk